In Love with Nature

Autumn

I'm going home the old way, with a light hand on the reins making the long approach. MAXINE KUMIN

My Book

We are in for a
spell of perfect
weather now, every day
luminous,
every night brimmed
with stars. 
Picnics at noon,
supper by the
applewood fire
at night,
a walk in the cool
moonlight
before bed.

Gladys Taber

FROM THE

Heart of the Home

AUTUMN

Susan Branch

Little, Brown and Company
New York • Boston

Little, Brown and Company
Time Warner Book Group
1271 Avenue of the Americas, New York, NY 10020
Visit our Web site at www.twbookmark.com

FIRST EDITION
ISBN 0-316-08866-8

Library of Congress Control Number
2004044168

10 9 8 7 6 5 4 3 2 1

RRD-IN

PRINTED IN THE
UNITED STATES OF AMERICA

DEDICATED TO

The Man Who Came To Dinner

JOE, OUT ON OUR MORNING WALK.

Did you know that Joe Hall, the love of my life, can cook? Oh yeah, he can cook; we do a kitchen dance like nobody's business! Many years ago I wrote in my diary that my perfect man would be a "6'2" Leo who can cook." And in came Joe. I met him in a restaurant in the fall; that winter he came to dinner, & we've never been apart since. This book is dedicated to my darling Joe, who makes Autumn very cozy for me (all the other seasons too!).

The
heart of
Autumn
Must have broken here,

And
poured its treasure
out upon the
leaves.
— Charlotte Fiske Bates

CONTENTS

AUTUMN ARTS 9
Decorating 10
Entertaining 12
"I Made It Myself" . . . 18
APPETIZERS 25
Harvest 38
SIDE DISHES . . . 41
Back-to-School . . . 59
THANKSGIVING . . . 62
Family Recipes . . . 64
MAIN DISHES . . 71
Morning Science 86
Leaf Peeping 89
SWEETS 91
Afternoon Tea 108
Cocktails 114
HALLOWEEN 115
Eat, Drink & Be Scary . . . 119
INDEX 125

"What is the use of a book," thought Alice,
"without pictures or conversations?"
Lewis Carroll

There is something in the autumn
that is native to my blood—
Touch of manner, hint of mood;
And my heart is like a rhyme,
With the yellow and the purple and
the crimson keeping time.

The scarlet of the maples can shake
me like a cry
Of bugles going by.
And my lonely spirit thrills
To see the frosty asters like a
smoke upon the hills.

There is something in October
sets the gypsy blood astir;
We must rise and follow her,
when from every hill of flame
She calls and calls
each vagabond by name.

Bliss Carman

I AM FOR EVERYTHING STARTING INTO FULL-BLOWN PERFECTION AT ONCE.
Susan Edmonstone Ferrier

Autumn Arts

She sang a song, a song of home,
A song that reach'd my heart.
Home, home, sweet, sweet home.
She sang the song of "Home Sweet Home",
The song that reach'd my heart.
Julian Jordan

DECORATING FOR AUTUMN

A whiff of woodsmoke on the wind, the first chill in the air, the woods just edged in gold & without looking at the calendar we know we've turned the page & it is September. Time to air the quilts, pick bouquets of sunflowers, light the first fire; time to put the "SWEET" in Home Sweet Home. ♥

Ah! There is nothing like Staying home for real comfort.
♥ JANE AUSTEN

WOODEN, PEWTER OR IRONSTONE BOWLS; A CORNUCOPIA FILLED WITH APPLES, POMEGRANATES, ACORNS, LEAVES, NUTS, ROSE HIPS, IVY, CHESTNUTS, PEARS, BITTERSWEET & CLEMENTINES.

AN OLD CLOCK THAT TICKS SOUNDS WONDERFUL

(ESPECIALLY WHEN THE ELECTRICITY GOES OUT). ♥

LAMPS ARE COZIER & MAKE A MUCH PRETTIER LIGHT THAN CEILING LIGHTS. ♥

LET THE LAST TOMATOES FROM THE GARDEN RIPEN ON A KITCHEN WINDOWSILL. ♥

DISPLAY OLD BOOKS
HEIDI
POLLYANNA
WUTHERING HEIGHTS
LITTLE WOMEN
ANNE OF GREEN GABLES
THE ADVENTURES OF HUCKLEBERRY FINN

GAMES & PUZZLES FOR COZY NIGHTS AT HOME. ♥

BREW MULLING SPICES, CINNAMON & SPICE AND EVERYTHING NICE. Have friends for Tea.

& ALL YOUR FAVORITES. ♥

We have a ledge over our front door ~ it's the perfect place for a row of small pumpkins...

They look cute on top of the kitchen cabinets too!

Fill the cookie jar & put tea cakes & muffins under glass.

Hang bunches of fresh herbs, pepperberries, yarrow & hydrangea. ♥

Make romance with fabric: Quilts make great table-cloths (add a ruffled lace "slip"). Plaid blankets & duvet covers, appliquéd felt blanket-stitched throw pillows, baskets of knitting, pillow-cases embroidered in fall motifs, bright-colored throws over couch & chairs, festive potholders, & old antique-store dish towels. ♥

Warm up the house with COLOR

RUST   BROWN

PURPLE   GREEN

DARK ORANGE GARNET

BURGUNDY   WARM YELLOW

Candles, candles, candles! Fires in the fireplace & outside ~ a bonfire ♥. Brass, wooden or pewter candleholders are perfect for the season. Sink a burgundy or dark orange pillar into sand in the bottom of a large hurricane lamp. Surround the candle with autumn windfall ~ tiny pinecones, leaves, berries, kumquats.

KITTY & DOG

A soft furry warm toasty friendly little petty-pet of your own is a must ♥.

Bring nature indoors.

Lots of votives in green or gold glass

"What a capital little house this is!" he called out cheerily. "So compact! So well planned! Everything here & everything in its place!" ♥ Kenneth Grahame

Entertaining...

LIFE CAN ALWAYS USE A LITTLE SPICING UP, SO GIVE A PARTY!

From the farewell-to-summer Labor Day picnic, to the harvest lunch, football feed & Thanksgiving dinner, Autumn offers all kinds of inspiration for fun. Here are some ideas to make entertaining more...well, ENTERTAINING.

Location, location, location! Set your table outdoors in the crisp air in the woods among the leaves. Have a party in a barn. Or have dinner in front of a cozy fire. We once served venison sausage directly from our in-fireplace grill ~ cooking over an open fire is an ancient appetite whetter.

Crowd folks around the dinner table. The closer they are to each other, the more intimate the conversation (the more Fun the dinner). Put 8 at a table for 6.

Lighting can add so much to a party — candles, candles everywhere! Make citrus votives (hollow out oranges, draw on a leaf & cut it out with a small sharp knife ~ pop in votive). Hurricane lamps outside, lanterns in trees, strings of tiny lights, tiki torches & if possible a bonfire ~ mmmmm.

Use the kookiest, prettiest, funnest, most interesting or elegant cocktail glasses you can find ~ dip rims in fruit juice & then into colored sugar.

12

Ask yourself: does it smell good, taste good, feel good, sound good & look good? Appeal to the senses.

Use molds to make butter or ice cubes shaped like leaves; you can also find crackers in leaf shapes.

Comfort food looks best served in pottery, wooden bowls (we have one, YES, shaped like a leaf!), pewter, ironstone, silver & brown & white transferware. Serving spoons with colorful handles, old wood spoons; I love our sterling silver baby spoon with bells on the handle. Bread looks best served in a basket.

I collect old cups & mugs & childrens' cups so everyone gets a different cup for after-dinner coffee. Mixing dish patterns makes things interesting.

Quilts make gorgeous tablecloths, but burlap or woolen blankets also look wonderful at an outside or barn party; layered old linen for Thanksgiving. Seating can be interesting too ~ hay bales for outside & old mix & match painted chairs look great indoors or out. For an intimate fireplace dinner, pull upholstered arm chairs up to the table.

Plan your menu ~ something simple & delicious & "make-ahead" ~ so you can be the unruffled hostess with the mostest & enjoy your own dinner party. We like Mrs. Calvin Coolidge, who after witnessing total disaster (a maid DROPPED the turkey), said calmly:

"Never mind, Mary, just take this turkey back to the kitchen & bring in the other one."

IF YOU'RE INTERESTED IN COOKING, YOU'RE ALSO JUST NATURALLY INTERESTED IN ART, IN LOVE, AND IN CULTURE.
Madame Jehane Benoit

The Autumn Table

Simple but interesting treatments for napkins & placecards can add lots of charm to special dinners. Dish towels make great napkins for picnics & messy dinners like lobster. Bring nature to the table ~ roll napkins & tie w/ grapevine, bittersweet, or ivy vines. Collect silver napkin rings & look for old linens. Use cotton, damask, or linen only ~ polyester does not absorb well & even seems to spit back. If you're expecting a crowd, fold napkins & make your placecards a few days before.

This little envelope napkin works for both casual & formal dinners. You can make them w/ homespun plaid napkins, Or they can be classically elegant when you iron crisp white linen as you fold. Check out napkin-folding books for more ideas.

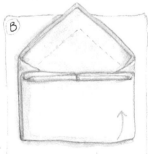

To FORM THE ENVELOPE:
(A) FOLD SQUARE NAPKIN IN HALF DIAGONALLY TO 1/8" FROM TOP. FOLD IN 2 BOTTOM CORNERS TO MEET IN CENTER. BRING IN SIDES TO MEET IN CENTER. (B) FOLD UP BOTTOM HALF OF NAPKIN TO JUST BELOW FLAP. (C) FOLD FLAP DOWN AS YOU WOULD AN ENVELOPE.

14

PLACECARDS

KARIS

Gather small (2"-3") dry leaves in different colors & shapes & write your guests' names on them in gold metallic pen, or a white "correction" type pen.

On pear-shaped write your guests' Icing (p.103). leas (or dry leas) icing into plastic a hole in corner & Practice writing on

Ginger Crisps (p.106), names in Royal Secure a fresh mint w/ a dot of icing. (Put sandwich bag, cut squeeze icing down. wax paper.)

Mary

Tie bundles of herbs w/ kitchen twine ~ cut out a tag w/ pinking shears. GOOD for a harvest lunch in the garden.

Katie

Enlarge old photos of friends on copier ~ use as placecard placemats.

TRICIA

~15~

MEET ME IN DREAMLAND, SWEET DREAMY DREAMLAND... *Beth Slater Whitson*

THE GUEST ROOM

COMPANY'S COMING! BRING THEIR LITTLE STRESSED-OUT SOULS INTO YOUR OWN LITTLE BIT OF HEAVEN.

Make the bed snug with fresh cotton sheets, a warm comforter, feather pillows, some cute pillow-cases for the season.

Fresh flowers: mums, marigolds, wild asters, rosehips or dahlias.

Bedside lamps, bottled water, clock, magazines; little books like *A Short Guide to a Happy Life* by Anna Quindlen.

Leave an empty spot in the closet & a few hangers.

Decorate with a basket of knitting, old toys, family photos & classic books.

Small windfall apples in a basket & a bowl of grapes.

A knitted nap blanket & a bathrobe.

Lavender sachets in dresser drawers (p. 19).

If you were to ask what is most important in a home, I would say memories. *Lillian Gish*

Whimsical & fun, or spiritual & solemn, traditions make memories ⚘ Light the fire & escape from reality with old movies: Mrs. Miniver, Camille, Love Letters, & The Quiet Man ⚘ Make popcorn balls & caramel apples ⚘ Read stories out loud before bed ⚘ Walk under the Hunter moon ⚘ Get together with friends & make wreaths for your doors ⚘ Have game night, book club, or knitting night ⚘ Write a long letter to someone you love ⚘ Fall spread-eagle into a pile of leaves ⚘ Lie in the leaves & listen to the church bells ring ⚘ Set out as many pictures as you can find of family members sitting on Santa's lap ⚘ Make holiday gifts ⚘ Have breakfast in bed ⚘ Make big soft molasses cookies ⚘ Give them in a basket with cider

MAKING MEMORIES
MY NEPHEW JESSE
HARVEST KING

TWIST 2 OR 3 RUNNERS OF ENGLISH IVY, GRAPEVINE, OR BITTERSWEET INTO A CIRCLE & BIND IT WITH FLORAL TAPE. INSERT FLOWERS & COLORFUL LEAVES, MARIGOLDS, MUMS, ROSE HIPS, OR PURPLE HYDRANGEAS.

·17·

I made it myself!

There is some- thing about Autumn that gets my creative juices flowing EVERYWHERE;

INSPIRATION IS

I think I'm still "back-to-school" strong urges to to put my photos harvest lunch & for it; plant out; tie up bunches apple butter; or like to walk & say to myself, are a few easy yourself a fun,

connecting to that feeling! I get MAKE something; in scrapbooks; plan a make the placecards bulbs, indoors & of herbs to dry; make sew something. I around my house "I made that." Here ways to give creative "fix."

Home Sweet Home is Homemade
in more ways than one~

WE COME BACK TO AUTUMN, TO ZUCCHINI THAT WILT LIKE WITCHES' SHOES.
MARGARET HASSE

EMBROIDERY

Easy

SIT IN FRONT OF A FIRE AND SEW UP SOME CHARMING LITTLE GIFTS, MAKE LITTLE PILLOWS, SACHETS, PINCUSHIONS, OR A STAR TO HANG. YOU NEED FABRIC: FELT IS GREAT, TRY QUILT REMNANTS, OR CHOOSE A FABRIC YOU LOVE. PUT IT IN A SEWING BASKET WITH EMBROIDERY THREAD, EMBROIDERY NEEDLES, PINS, RIBBON TO HANG PROJECTS WITH; BUTTONS TO DECORATE IF YOU LIKE, AND STUFFING TO PLUMP THINGS UP.

2004

Here's How... **C**UT DOUBLED FABRIC INTO DESIRED SHAPE (SO YOU HAVE A BACK & A FRONT). PIN IT & BLANKET-STITCH IT 3/4 OF THE WAY &...

And finish off with the **BLANKET STITCH**

FILL IT WITH

Lavender Flowers, **BALSAM,** *Or* *Cotton Batting*

BRING THREAD THROUGH FABRIC AT A, HOLD THREAD W/ THUMB; GO DOWN AT B AND UP AT C, WITH NEEDLE OVER THREAD~ PULL INTO PLACE. USE THE RUNNING STITCH TO EMBROIDER YOUR NAME & THE DATE ON YOUR PROJECT.

GIFT BASKETS

CHANNEL SOME OF THAT CREATIVE ENERGY
INTO HOLIDAY & HOUSEWARMING GIFTS.

The gathering together of the perfect ingredients for gift baskets (or other fun containers) is just as much fun as being on the receiving end of such personal attention. After all, 'tis (ALMOST) the season———!

Cocoa Cup

COCOA MIX (P. 111) WITH HOMEMADE MARSHMALLOWS (P. 110) & A SPECIAL CUP. TIE RECIPE TO THE CUP HANDLE.

Cookie Basket

FILL A BASKET W/ UNFROSTED COOKIE CUTTER COOKIES. ADD DECORATING SUPPLIES: ROYAL ICING (P. 103), FOOD COLORING & LITTLE CANDIES.

SNIFFLE BASKET

HOMEMADE CHICKEN SOUP (P. 56), THE BOOK _ENCHANTED APRIL_ & THE INGREDIENTS FOR FAMOUS COLD "MEDICINE" RECIPE: INTO CUP OF BOILING WATER ADD JUICE OF ONE LEMON, 1 TBSP. HONEY & A SHOT WHISKEY. (Say Goodnight!)

Sock Neck Warmer

FLU CHASER
FILL A CUTE KNEE-HIGH SOCK W/ UNCOOKED RICE. TIE THE OPEN END CLOSED W/ A RIBBON. HEAT IT IN MICROWAVE FOR 1 MIN. & PLACE IT AROUND BACK OF NECK. MMMMM

Apple Bowl

An old mixing bowl & wooden spoon, 4 green apples & in the bottom of the bowl, a bag of fresh cranberries & a plastic bag with all the dry ingred. measured out for Cranberry Apple Crisp (P. 95). Tie recipe to the spoon.

Sunday Breakfast

Into an old-fashioned batter bowl: pancake mix, real maple syrup, 2 bananas, whisk & dish towel.

15"

12"

Cookie Man

First measure out all dry ingred. for Ginger Crisps on p. 106. Combine sugars in one reclosable plastic bag & the rest of dry ingred. in another. Set aside. With pinking shears, cut out cookie man from 2 layers of heavy brown paper. On one (the "front"), sew on buttons & draw on mouth w/ red crayon. On the "back", write out the cookie recipe "cream 1 c. butter w/ sugars," etc. Include baking instructions. On a sewing machine, w/ red thread, sew the 2 sides together, leaving the head open. Place flattened bags of dry ingred. inside Cookie Man. Sew head closed. Punch a hole in his hand & tie on a cookie cutter. Sign & date the back!

It's Christmas in the heart that puts Christmas in the air. W.T. Ellis

·21·

MY HOUSE

My house in New England is on an island off the coast of Massachusetts and was built in 1849 by a whaling captain. His name was Smith, which Joe & I like, because both of our mothers' maiden names are Smith too. Many families have called this place **HOME**, & I can feel their presence here. When I pull down my big yellow bowl to make my grandma's turkey stuffing, I think of all the good things cooked up in this kitchen (before there were even refrigerators!): fresh eggs & milk, boiled lobsters, wild turkeys & roast pig; sweet corn & string beans from the garden; fresh-churned butter, homemade biscuits & buckwheat cakes; fried chicken, cornbread & apple dumplings. I imagine the lives lived here; new babies, weddings, welcome homes & fare-thee-wells through the generations. Daily life was so quiet when this house was born. Instead of T.V., telephone & boom box noises, there was the clip-clop of horses, the jangle of wagons, the sound of wood being split & the sweet music of birds singing & children playing.

As we sit in front of the fireplace on chilly fall evenings, listening to the wind blow outside, I often imagine other evenings in other times, what the room must have looked like then,

all in candlelight & firelight, what the people would have been wearing, what their lives were like, how they spent their time. How was it in 1853? 1882? 1906? 1939? I wish the fireplace would speak to me.

The house is tall & plain, white with dark green shutters. It doesn't have a garage, it has a barn. Near the kitchen door is a pole w/an iron horse head on it where a horse & buggy could be hitched. The garden is old too, & the roots go way down. There are 3 huge linden trees that almost touch the stars. The yard is all in colors now; the leaves are already off the birch trees but the maples are on fire. There's a church with a tall spire just across the street & behind it, a beautiful old graveyard. It's a short walk, 3 blocks (downhill), to the sea, through a neighborhood of old houses, rose arbors & garden gates. Most of the doors have Indian corn on them now; there are pumpkins on porches festooned with American flags & the air is filled with swirling leaves. In my house, here in the room that was known to other generations as "the music room," I write & watercolor books on cooking & babies & love & other things. Yesterday I left my art table & went to the back-yard late in the afternoon. There was a breezy little chill in the air, but it was still warm in the sun so I lay in the grass with my ear to the ground, thinking I could hear a heartbeat from the earth, & my kitty came & rolled over on his back & we lay there like comrades, looking up into the blue sky & tall trees, watching the leaves drift down. We JUMPED, a little startled, when the bells from the old church across the street suddenly began to ring. We looked at each other & smiled.

THIS IS THE BEST DAY THE WORLD HAS EVER SEEN. TOMORROW WILL BE BETTER. R.A. Campbell

In the village store someone
says, "I heard the geese go over," and
there is a moment of silence.
Why this is so moving,
I do not know.
But all of us feel it.

GLADYS TABER

Appetizers and Finger Food

Summer's loss seems
little, dear, on days
like these. ERNEST DOWSON

'TIS THE SEASON

Invite all your favorite people over, show 'em your creative side (someone has to be the inspiration!) ~ get connected! It's "dinner-party season;" check out the cocktails on p.114 & serve them with these quick & easy appetizer ideas & recipes for all occasions.

Hollow out a small round loaf of sourdough bread & fill it with all kinds of delicious olives. Set it on a bed of rosemary. Use a smaller roll for the pits. Fill other rolls with creamy cheeses.

Look for leaf-shaped crackers to serve with dips & spreads.
"Terra Chips" are vegetable chips & come in all the colors of the season, orange, purple, gold & red ~ look great in baskets.

Find a giant margarita glass (Sur la Table sells them), rim the glass w/ lime juice & dip it in coarse salt. Fill it with guacamole, hang a slice of lime over the edge & serve w/ lime-flavored tortilla chips. (See p.114 for another way to use this fun vessel)

If you have access to game, cook elk or deer sausage in your fireplace (there are special fireplace grills available at kitchen shops) ~ have hot 'n' spicy & honey mustard.

Use lemon or grape leaves to line butter dishes & serving platters.

...And merry when the great winds
through autumn's woodlands sing,
brown...
—William Hewitt

26

SPICED PECANS

350° Makes 2 cups

Impossible to eat just one!
Great on salads. Pack them into old jars
and they make a wonderful gift.

spray olive oil
2 c. pecan halves
1/4 c. brown sugar,
    firmly packed

1/4 c. melted butter
4 tsp. Mexican hot
    pepper sauce (CHOLULA)
1 tsp. salt
1/2 tsp. black pepper

Preheat oven to 350°. Lightly spray olive oil on a cookie
sheet. Mix all other ingred. & spread on pan in 1 layer.
Bake 10 min. until lightly toasted, stirring once. Cool.

GARLIC SHRIMP

Makes approx. 50 shrimp

Fast in the microwave. Serve with Garlic Tomato Bread (p. 34).

1-2lb. bag lg. (21-30 per. lb.)
    frozen, cooked, ready-to-
    eat shrimp
1/2 c. minced flat-leaf parsley

2-3 cloves garlic
3 tbsp. butter
pinch cayenne pepper

Thaw shrimp, rinse well & pat dry. Put them in a bowl.
Pile minced garlic on top; put 1 tbsp. butter on top of
garlic; dot rest of butter over shrimp. Microwave on high
1 minute, stir well, make sure they're hot, sprinkle lightly
w/cayenne & add parsley. Stir well again & serve.

27

Figs & Goat Cheese (Lusciousness!)

You'll need fresh Mission figs, creamy goat cheese, half-cooked bacon, fresh rosemary sprigs. Cut off top 1/3 of each fig, reserving tops. With melon baller, make a hollow in the top of each fig; fill w/ goat cheese, put tops back on & wrap each w/ partially cooked bacon. Secure w/ rosemary sprig (or toothpick). Broil until bacon is cooked through & serve immediately. (P.S. You DO eat the skin on a fig.)

Wild Mushroom Toast:

Cut rounds of rye bread, lay them on cookie sheets & toast under broiler. Turn them over, butter untoasted side & top w/ hot Wild Mushroom Ragout (p. 53). Sprinkle over Parmesan cheese. Also good on garlic bread.

Gorgonzola Cream:

Mix together softened cream cheese & enough gorgonzola cheese to flavor it lightly (or to your taste). Serve w/ crusty hot bread; make balls & roll in minced walnuts; stuff it in celery; put a dollop on a walnut half; mold it around a grape & roll in minced pecans; spread it on pear slices.

Baby BLT's:

Cut rounds of sourdough bread, lay them on cookie sheet & toast under broiler. Turn them over & top each piece w/ a slice of cherry tomato, salt & pepper, a dollop of mayonnaise & a piece of bacon on top.

Prosciutto Pears:

Wrap thin pieces of prosciutto around juicy-ripe pear slices.

I FIGURE YOU HAVE THE SAME CHANCE OF WINNING THE LOTTERY WHETHER YOU PLAY OR NOT. — Fran Lebowitz

YOU CAN OFFER THEM A VEGETABLE PLATE, & YOU SHOULD, BUT THIS IS WHAT THEY REALLY WANT! THERE'S A TIME & PLACE FOR EVERYTHING; ♥ A RAINY, WINDY, COZY DAY WITH A FOOTBALL GAME OR OLD MOVIE ON TV IS THE TIME FOR…

Red Chili Onion Rings!

Serves 1-6 (it depends!)

2 lg. yellow onions, peeled & sliced into thin rings

1½ c. whole milk

2-3 c. canola oil

1 c. flour

2 Tbsp. paprika

1 Tbsp. good chili powder

1 tsp. cayenne

1 tsp. salt

more salt to taste

Soak onion rings in milk for ½ hr. Heat oil to about 350°. Mix together next 5 ingred. Drain onions & toss in flour mixture. Fry in oil 'til golden. Drain on paper towels, season w/ salt & serve. (NOTE: don't dredge onions in flour until you are ready to fry them.)

Potato Bar

Makes 24 pieces

MAKE CRISPY POTATO BOATS, SERVE W/ A VARIETY OF "MAKE-YOUR-OWN" CONDIMENTS, & YOU WILL HAVE THE MOST POPULAR HOUSE IN TOWN ♥.

6 lg. baking potatoes

canola oil

½ c. melted butter

salt & pepper

paprika

shredded cheese ★

Preheat oven to 425°. Wash & dry potatoes; rub all over w/ oil; prick w/ fork, put potatoes in oven; reduce heat to 350° & bake 1 hr. When tender, cut lengthwise in quarters. Scoop out pulp, leaving a ¼" "boat" for fillings. Brush both sides of potato w/ butter; season w/ s & p, & paprika. Bake skin side up, 15 min., turn & bake 10 min. more. Remove from oven, fill with cheese (★ smoked gouda, cheddar, fontina, pepper jack, etc.) & reheat to melt cheese. Condiments: set out bowls of bacon, sour cream, green onions, salsa, red pepper flakes, avocado, cilantro, cooked chicken & ham.

Crunchy Chicken

450° about 50 pieces

Football-fans-tested & approved. Score!

3 Dips

1 med. bag potato chips
1/4 tsp. cayenne
1/4 tsp. salt
2 lg. eggs
2 lb. boneless, skinless chicken breasts or thighs

1/2 c. sweet chili sauce, store-bought
1 c. sour cream
1/2 c. salsa
1/2 c. whole-grain mustard

Preheat oven to 450° & spray cookie sheet w/oil. Crush 1/2 the potato chips finely w/rolling pin, & the rest into very small pieces. Stir in cayenne & salt. Whisk eggs together. Wash chicken & cut into 1 1/2" "bites." Dip chicken pieces into egg; firmly press into potato chips & place in one layer on cookie sheet. Bake 10 min. Put chili sauce in a dipping bowl; divide the sour cream into 2 other bowls. Stir the mustard into one & salsa into the other. Serve.

IF A MAN WATCHES MORE THAN 3 FOOTBALL GAMES IN A ROW HE SHOULD BE DECLARED LEGALLY DEAD. Erma Bombeck

STICKY SHRIMP
With Asian Dipping Sauce

Makes about 50 pieces

1 c. rice wine vinegar
3 tbsp. light soy sauce
2 tsp. toasted sesame oil
1 tsp. chili garlic sauce
2 tsp. minced fresh ginger
1 lb. raw shrimp (21-30 per lb.)
 peeled, deveined, tails off

3/4 c. pineapple juice
1 egg
1¼ c. flour
veg. oil for frying
2-7 oz. bags (5 c.) shredded
 coconut (sweetened)

Combine first 5 ingred. (chili garlic sauce is in the Asian section of the market); cover & chill. Cut each shrimp in half lengthwise. Combine juice w/egg, gradually stir in flour until smooth. Heat 1½" veg. oil in lg. skillet. Put coconut in shallow bowl. Dip shrimp in batter, then coat w/coconut. Fry a few at a time about 3 min., 'til golden on both sides. Drain on paper towels. (You can make them 1 day ahead, refrigerate & then reheat in 350° oven.) Serve with dipping sauce.

IF I EVER HAVE TIME FOR THE THINGS THAT MATTER,
 IF EVER I HAVE THE SMALLEST CHANCE,
I'M GOING TO LIVE IN
LITTLE BROOM GARDENS,
MOAT-BY-THE-CASTLE,
NETTLECOMB, HANTS.
Vilda Sauvage Owens

ALL THE WAY
TO HEAVEN
IS HEAVEN. ♥
ST. CATHERINE
OF SIENA

Stuffed New Potatoes

TINY NEW POTATOES
SALT
FRESHLY GROUND PEPPER
ONION POWDER
FONTINA CHEESE
PAPRIKA
CHIVES or GREEN ONION

Preheat broiler to 500°. Cook potatoes in salted water 'til tender. Cool, cut each in half & with small end of melon baller carefully make a little hollow in each half. Put them on a baking sheet ~ liberally salt & pepper & sprinkle with onion powder. Fill cavities w/ shredded fontina, sprinkle w/ paprika; broil about 5 min.'til toasty brown. Remove from oven & garnish w/ fresh chives or minced green onion.

Savory Sage Riblets

375°   Serves a bunch

Crunchy, spicy, chewy ribs everyone LOVES.

2½ tsp. ground sage
2½ tsp. salt
2½ tsp. black pepper

1¼ tsp. thyme
1¼ tsp. onion powder
¼ + ⅛ tsp. cayenne
6 lbs. baby back ribs

Preheat oven to 375°. Blend together first 6 ingred. Rub mixture over both sides of ribs. Put them on a baking sheet; roast ½ hr., turn & cook 1 hr. more.

BUTTERNUT SHOTGLASS SOUP

If you are someone who has a great collection of shotglasses ~ this is the recipe for you! If not, they are inexpensive & this is such a fun presentation ~ guests oooh & aaah when they see a tray of soup being passed.

MAKES 10 CUPS

3 Tbsp. butter
1 lg. onion, chopped
2 carrots, sliced
2 med. potatoes, peeled & cubed
2½ lbs. butternut squash, peeled & cubed

6 c. chicken stock (canned, or p. 56)
1½ tsp. curry
pinch each: nutmeg & ginger
GARNISHES: sour cream, or croutons (p. 34), or grated asiago cheese

Melt butter in soup pot, sauté onion & carrots until soft; stir in potatoes & squash. Add stock, bring to boil, reduce heat & simmer, partially covered, for 40 min. Add curry, nutmeg & ginger. Purée soup in batches in blender or food processor. Return to saucepan, add salt & pepper to taste. Fill shotglasses, add your garnish of choice & pass to guests on a tray.

I AM TWO WITH NATURE. Woody Allen

33

Butter-Bit Croutons

You must know by now, details ~ those special little touches that make things interesting. These tiny, crunchy croutons are wonderful over salads, soups & casseroles, (& to eat straight from the jar!); they keep well & make a great gift (in, for instance, an old mortar & pestle or other interesting container).

5-6 slices white sandwich
    bread (not sourdough)
3 Tbsp. butter
salt

Stack up the bread slices. With a serrated knife, cut off crusts & discard. Hold bread firmly & cut into 1/4" cubes. Melt butter & quickly add bread cubes to butter ~ stir so all bits get buttery. Toast over med. heat 'til golden brown, stirring often. Drain on paper towels, sprinkle w/salt.

Garlic Tomato Bread

Spoon this on hot, crusty French bread ~ makes 2 cups.

1-28 oz. can peeled, whole tomatoes   2 tsp. balsamic vinegar
3 cloves garlic, minced   2 Tbsp. chopped fresh basil
2 Tbsp. olive oil   1/4 tsp. salt

Pour off juice from tomatoes. Break them up or cut them into bite-size pieces, discarding stems; put in bowl. Pour off almost all the juice & stir in all other ingred. Let sit 1 hour. Chill before serving.

34

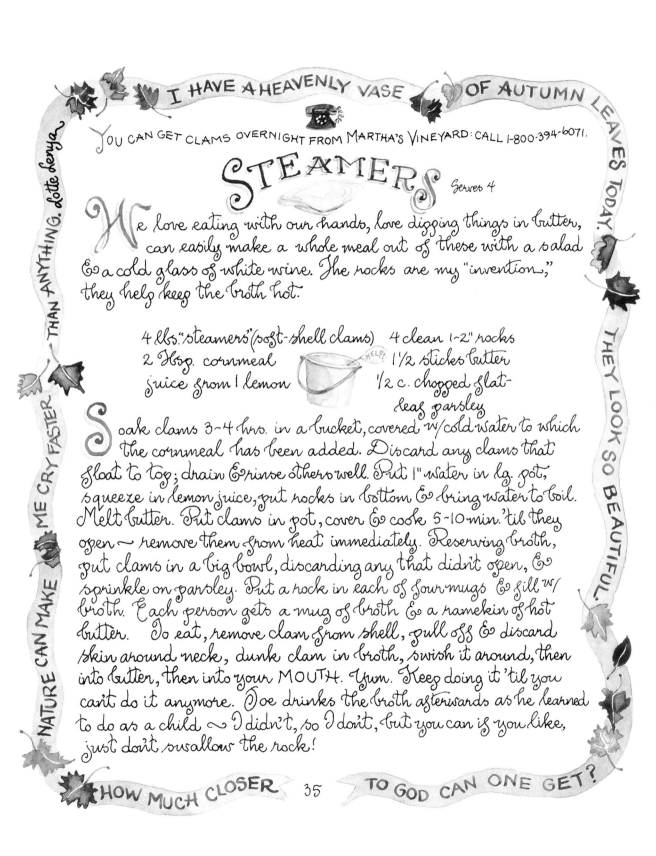

YOU CAN GET CLAMS OVERNIGHT FROM MARTHA'S VINEYARD: CALL 1-800-394-6071.

STEAMERS

Serves 4

We love eating with our hands, love digging things in butter, can easily make a whole meal out of these with a salad & a cold glass of white wine. The rocks are my "invention," they help keep the broth hot.

4 lbs. "steamers" (soft-shell clams)   4 clean 1-2" rocks
2 Tbsp. cornmeal   1½ sticks butter
juice from 1 lemon   ½ c. chopped flat-
                                          leaf parsley

Soak clams 3-4 hrs. in a bucket, covered w/ cold water to which the cornmeal has been added. Discard any clams that float to top; drain & rinse others well. Put 1" water in lg. pot, squeeze in lemon juice, put rocks in bottom & bring water to boil. Melt butter. Put clams in pot, cover & cook 5-10 min. 'til they open ～ remove them from heat immediately. Reserving broth, put clams in a big bowl, discarding any that didn't open, & sprinkle on parsley. Put a rock in each of four mugs & fill w/ broth. Each person gets a mug of broth & a ramekin of hot butter.   To eat, remove clam from shell, pull off & discard skin around neck, dunk clam in broth, swish it around, then into butter, then into your MOUTH. Yum. Keep doing it 'til you can't do it anymore. Joe drinks the broth afterwards as he learned to do as a child ～ I didn't, so I don't, but you can if you like, just don't swallow the rock!

FRUIT and CHEESE with ORANGE DIP

On a wooden tray arrange slices of Asian pears, red pears & black & red seedless grapes. Include a small wheel of Saga blue cheese & a little pottery bowl filled w/ Orange Dip (for the pears). Makes ¾ c.

2 tbsp. lemon juice	3 tbsp. orange juice concentrate
⅓ c. sour cream	zest & juice of 1 orange
⅓ c. mayonnaise	1 tsp. ground ginger

Drizzle pears w/ lemon juice. Whisk all other ingred. together — reserve a little zest to garnish dip. Serve dip & fruit chilled; cheese should be room temp.

AVOCADO and GRAPEFRUIT SPEARS

Roughly mash avocados w/ a fork. "Dice" fresh red grapefruit segments. Thin some mayonnaise w/ grapefruit juice ('til "drizzleable"). Spread avocado on red & green Belgian endive spears. Put 2 or 3 pieces of grapefruit on each. Drizzle w/ mayo sauce & sprinkle each w/ 2 or 3 pomegranate seeds. Chill.

DON'T FORGET: STUFFED MUSHROOMS!

For another delicious appetizer, stuff "baby bells" (small Portabello mushrooms) w/ mixture on p. 52 & cook 5-8 min.

AUTUMN IS THE BEST SEASON IN WHICH TO SNIFF, AND TO SNIFF FOR PLEASURE, FOR THIS IS THE SEASON OF UNIVERSAL PUNGENCY. Bertha Damon

INDIAN SHUCK BREAD

Serves 6

corn husks ✤
2 c. yellow cornmeal
1 Tbsp. brown sugar
1 tsp. cinnamon

1 tsp. baking powder
½ tsp. salt
¼ tsp. cayenne
MAPLE BUTTER (below)

You can use inner husks from 12 ears of fresh corn or buy a bag of corn husks ~ in our store they're right next to the tortillas. Soak husks in water for 1 hr. Stir together next 6 ingred. Add 1½ c. boiling water, mix well. Form mixture into little rolls (12 or more), wrap in corn husks ~ tear off strips of husk & use to tie ends ✄. Drop rolls in boiling water & cook 10 min. Serve hot in husks with

MAPLE BUTTER

Cream together 1 c. soft butter, ¼ c. maple syrup & ½ tsp. Mexican hot pepper sauce (Cholula).

All American Indian poems are songs, & an Indian was once asked which came first, the words or the music. "They came together," he replied.

Marie Gilchrist

Life begins the day you start a garden — Chinese Proverb

Harvest

I made my garden small because I didn't want the thing I adore to turn into a chore! But small is good; when I fill my garden basket with my own tomatoes, lemon cucumbers, purple potatoes & tie up old-fashioned herbs like rosemary, thyme & sage, I get to feel a small part of the ancient cycle of reaping & sowing. We grow different things every year — this year my favorite herb was lemon thyme. It is so wonderful, delicious in everything it touches, has little flowers you can even stir into softened vanilla ice cream. So good! If you don't have it now, there is always next year. And be sure to plant white Cosmos next summer; Cosmos blooms 'til first freeze & looks like wildflowers growing over the garden fence. And your kitty would love a soft bed of catnip to roll in while you garden. Don't forget lavender! Delicious in tea cakes & cookies; moths don't like it so it makes perfect sachets for your linen closet. Gardens are heaven — gardens & churches have a lot in common.

THERE CAN BE NO OTHER OCCUPATION LIKE GARDENING IN WHICH, IF YOU WERE TO CREEP UP BEHIND SOMEONE AT THEIR WORK, YOU WOULD FIND THEM SMILING. — Mirabel Osler

To PLANT A SEED IS A HOPEFUL DEED.

THE GOD OF MUSIC DWELLETH OUT OF DOORS.
Edith Thomas

Blueberries from Chile? Basil from Thailand? Lettuce from Mexico? Yup, & labels are not required to tell us where our food comes from, or what the laws are about food safety in those countries. A good rule of thumb is "the closer to home your food is grown, the better it will be." When you grow your own 🥕🍅, you know where they come from, you know they're fresh & you know they aren't covered in pesticides. It would probably be a full-time job becoming organic everything, but every little bit helps. And new local farms are springing up all over the country where there are not only vegetables, but chickens, pigs & lambs for organic eggs & meat. Farmers markets & farm co-ops are empowering us to feel closer to our earth & our food.

Around here, a visit to the charming Morning 🌼 Glory Farm is an end-of-season must; harvest vegetables & fruit to can & freeze for winter; wreaths, scarecrows, dried corn, bittersweet, grapevine & pumpkins galore. 🎃 We leave munching their still-warm zucchini bread & take our pumpkins home to set out in the garden. 🍁

My vegetables don't speak to me in words, but we are in communication. Before I harvest them to take them to the market, I always say, "Thank you so much, you sweeties."
Elizabeth Berry

39

Harvest Kitchen

THE GREEKS HAD JUST ONE WORD FOR "ECONOMIZE." OUR
NEW ENGLAND GRANDMOTHERS HAD TWELVE: "EAT IT UP; USE
IT UP; MAKE DO; OR DO WITH OUT." *Helen Adamson*

WE EAT WHAT WE CAN, & WHAT
WE CAN'T, WE CAN. *My Grandma*

SIDE DISHES

THE BEST "AROMATHERAPY" COMES DIRECTLY FROM THE KITCHEN. ♥

Acorn Squash

Preheat oven to 400°. Allow one squash for 2 people. Cut squash in half widthwise & place facedown on baking sheet. Bake 40 min. 'til soft. Remove from oven, turn halves over. Into each cavity put:

1 Tbsp. butter
1 Tbsp. brown sugar
1 Tbsp. golden raisins
a sprinkle of cinnamon

Put squash back into oven 5 min. Remove from oven & fluff w/ fork. For extra prettiness, garnish each w/ ½ chopped red pear.

Garnishes

Put a little extra charm in your dinner parties. Have fun w/ cookie cutters & garnish soups, salads, vegetable dishes & even drinks w/ food cutouts: potatoes in leaf shapes (see p. 44); you can make star, heart, or snowflake-shaped beets, apples, croutons, bell peppers, sweet potatoes, & don't forget starfruit.

Excellent potatoes, smoking hot, and accompanied by melted butter of the first quality, would alone stamp merit on any dinner.... Thomas Walker

Make "EXCELLENT POTATOES" EVEN MORE EXCELLENT BY RUBBING SKIN WITH SOFTENED BUTTER & SALTING BEFORE BAKING. ♥

Steamed or roasted asparagus, green beans, artichokes, broccoli, cauliflower, or Brussels sprouts are all delicious with

Joe's Famous Hollandaise

¾ c. Serves 6

1 stick butter
juice of ½ lemon
2 extra lg. eggs, yolks only
pinch of cayenne
pinch of white pepper

Melt butter in sm. saucepan, remove from heat & squeeze in lemon juice. In the top part of double boiler, whisk egg yolks 'til warmed. Drizzle in butter little by little, whisking constantly. Remove from heat, add cayenne & pepper. Pour over vegetables & serve.

ROASTED FALL VEGETABLES

THIS RECIPE IS SO EASY ~ & SO GOOD! HEAVEN W/ ROASTS & CHOPS.

per person, approx:

1 leek, white part only
2 shallots, peeled
2-3 new potatoes (red, purple & brown)

2-3 thin carrots, halved
1 piece of fennel
4 shitake mushrooms
olive oil
Caramelized Onion Sauce (below)

Preheat oven to 400°. Put a lg. pot of water on to boil. Oil a lg. roasting pan. Clean leeks (slit them down the middle & let water run through) & put them, along w/ shallots, into roasting pan; brush w/ a bit of olive oil; put pan in oven. Put the potatoes, carrots, & fennel into boiling water; as they become tender, pull them out of water, dry them, brush w/ oil & add them to roasting pan. Add mushrooms. Continue roasting veg. about 20 min. more 'til tender & golden. (Total roasting time for shallots is 45 min. to 1 hr.) Spoon onion sauce over the vegetables & serve.

CARAMELIZED ONION SAUCE

MAKES 2 C. ~ ENOUGH TO SERVE 6

4 Tbsp. olive oil
4 med. onions, halved & thinly sliced
3 cloves garlic, minced

1/4 c. + 3 Tbsp. balsamic vinegar (at least 10 years old if possible)
1 Tbsp. + 1 tsp. brown sugar
salt to taste

Heat 1 Tbsp. of the oil in lg. skillet. Cook onions, stirring often, for about 1/2 hr., 'til light brown. Add garlic, cook 1 min. Stir in remaining 3 Tbsp. oil, vinegar & sugar. Cook 2 min. more. Sprinkle w/ salt to taste.

Potatoes Anna
'Specially for Autumn
425° – 500°   Serves 8

Beautiful layers of buttery-crisp potatoes turned onto a platter & covered w/ sweet potato & purple potato
leaves ~ GORGEOUS!

1 or 2 leaf-shaped cookie cutters	1 lg. yam
1 stick butter	2 biggest purple (new)
7 lg. Idaho potatoes	potatoes
	salt & pepper

Preheat oven to 425°. Melt butter; when it begins to sizzle, remove
from heat & skim off foamy white stuff on top. Set aside what's left
("clarified butter" doesn't burn as easily). Put aside the biggest Idaho
potato along w/ the yam & purple potatoes. Peel remaining 6 Idaho potatoes &
thinly slice (1/16"); put them in a bowl of cold water. Put 1-2 tbsp. clarified butter
in a lg. oven-proof skillet (around 11"). Dry each round w/ paper towels as you
go (very important) & line the bottom of the pan w/ overlapping slices. Brush
all w/ butter, sprinkle on s & p & continue w/ a 2nd layer ~ fill pan to
very top, press down w/ spatula. Bake 50 min., press down again during
baking. Turn heat up to 500° & cook 10 min. more. Gently loosen edge
w/ knife, turn out on platter, decorate w/ Potato Leaves & serve. While
potatoes bake, make

Potato Leaves

Peel remaining potatoes ~ thinly cut lengthwise to have widest slices
possible ~ Cut out leaf shapes w/ cookie cutter. Fry them well in a little
oil & butter, s & p all, & sprinkle paprika on some. When brown-
edged & done, drain on paper towels. Leaves can be made ahead.

THIS TIME, WHEN HIS HEART LEAPT,
TO LEAP TOO, LIKE A LITTLE COLT

SOMETHING ~ HIS SOUL ~ SEEMED
INVITED OUT OF A PEN.
— Eudora Welty

Roasted Beet Salad

425° Serves 6

2 heads romaine, washed & dried
6 med. beets
olive oil

1 lg. red onion, thinly sliced
Blue Cheese Dressing (below)
3/4 c. chopped walnuts
Butter-Bit Croutons (p. 34)

Preheat oven to 425°. Chill lettuce. Wash & dry beets; Trim roots & all but 1" of stems (leave skins on). Put beets in a shallow baking dish, drizzle w/oil, cover w/ foil & roast about 1 hr. 'til tender. Cool; peel them & cut into bite-sized pieces. Chill. MAKE CROUTONS & DRESSING.

To Serve:
On each salad plate put a handful of torn romaine & then roasted beets. Scatter onion over top. Spoon on dressing (be sure to get lots of cheese!). Sprinkle walnuts over, then croutons & serve. ♡

Creamy & Mild Blue Cheese DRESSING

THIS IS THE BEST STUFF!
YOU WILL BE TEMPTED TO DO A SWAN DIVE INTO THE BOWL.

4 oz. soft, mild blue cheese
1/2 c. sour cream
2 tbsp. half & half

1 tsp. cider vinegar
1/4 c. mayonnaise
2 tbsp. blue cheese crumbles

POUR INTO BOWL.

Into blender put 1st 4 ingred. ~ Blend 'til smooth, Whisk in mayo; stir in cheese crumbles. Chill. Stir well before serving.

TALKING? IT'S THE MOST LOQUACIOUS OF ALL.

What's the difference between ignorance & arrogance? I don't know & I don't care. ♡

POTLUCK BLUE RIBBON
Pecan Spinach Toss
Serves 8-10

A highly satisfactory cooking project, light, fragrant & special. (You can use plain raw pecans if you feel the need for speed.)

1 c. Spiced Pecans (p.27) coarsely chopped

2 c. orzo (1 lb.)

8 c. boiling water

5 c. chopped fresh baby spinach leaves

5 oz. (1¼ c.) crumbled feta cheese (soft mild sheep's milk)

1½ Tbsp. olive oil

2 tsp. lemon zest

1½ Tbsp. fresh lemon juice

½ Tsp. salt

Make pecans & set aside. Add orzo to boiling water, cook 6 min. Rinse in cold water & drain well. Put spinach, crumbled cheese & pecans in a lg. bowl & add orzo. Mix together last 4 ingred. ~ pour over salad & toss well.

Even in her childhood she extracted from life double enjoyment that comes usually only to the creative mind. "Now I am doing this. Now I am doing that," she told herself while she was doing it. Looking on while she participated. ♪ Edna Ferber

46

Red Pear, Black Grape, Spiced Pecan Salad

Serves 8

Lots of red, very festive & pretty.

Spiced Pecans (p. 27)
3/4 c. balsamic vinegar (aged)
1/2 c. olive oil
6 Tbsp. brown sugar
salt & pepper
1 lb. red leaf lettuce, butter
lettuce or baby spinach

1 pomegranate, seeded
the biggest, darkest seedless
grapes you can find, halved
1 lg. red onion, thinly sliced rings
1/2 c. crumbled blue cheese
4 ripe red pears
zest of 2 oranges

Make pecans, set aside. In a small saucepan, blend next 4 ingred.; stir over med. heat 'til sugar dissolves; set aside. Divide torn greens among 8 salad plates. Scatter over pomegranate seeds, arrange 10 grape halves, skin side up, over greens. Scatter onion rings & blue cheese. Halve pears, core & cut into 1/2" slices — put a pear half, skin side up, in the center of each salad. Arrange pecans; drizzle w/reserved dressing. Dust top of each salad w/ orange zest. Serve.

Give me the splendid silent sun with all his beams full-dazzling, give me juicy autumnal fruit ripe and red from the orchard. Walt Whitman

Warm Salad of White Beans, Sage & Garlic

SERVES 6

All warm & herbal, full of gentle flavors; take it to a potluck or Labor Day picnic.

9 oz. small white beans (dried)
1/4 c. minced fresh sage
1 tsp. minced garlic
3 Tbsp. minced flat-leaf parsley

1/3 c. olive oil
1 Tbsp. balsamic vinegar
1/2 tsp. salt
1 stalk celery, finely chopped
s & p to taste
arugula leaves (opt.)

Sort, rinse & drain beans. Bring them to a boil in 4 c. water; reduce heat & simmer 5 min. Remove from heat, cover & let sit 1 hr. Rinse beans & return to pan w/ 8 c. fresh water. Simmer 20 min. so beans are tender, not mushy. Rinse again in hot water & drain. Put in bowl. Mix together sage, garlic, parsley, oil, vinegar & salt & pour over beans; stir gently; let sit 1/2 hr. Add celery & taste for seasoning. Serve warm or at room temp. & pretty on a bed of arugula.

WE MADE A BONFIRE OF PINE BRANCHES AND FALLEN LEAVES & STOOD AROUND SNIFFING IT WITH PLEASURE UNTIL THERE WERE ONLY ASHES.

BUTTERMILK
MASHED POTATOES

Serves 8

10 med. baking potatoes, peeled & halved
10 whole cloves garlic, peeled

1½ c. buttermilk
½ c. minced parsley
salt & pepper to taste

Drop potatoes & garlic into a lg. pot of boiling water & cook until potatoes are fork tender. Drain & mash potatoes & garlic together with remaining ingred. Serve.

BOURBON MASHED
SWEET POTATOES

375° Serves 8

5 lbs. sweet potatoes (yams)
½ stick butter
¼ c. bourbon

¼ c. brown sugar
zest of one orange
salt & pepper to taste

Preheat oven to 375°. Pierce potatoes & bake 1-1½ hrs., 'til soft. Let cool 15 min. Halve potatoes & scoop pulp into lg. bowl. Partially mash ~ add remaining ingred., mash well & serve.

Keep potatoes warm for hours in top part of double boiler over very low heat (covered).

49

Balsamic Syrup

Yummy! Drizzle over veggies, steak & even fruit. Simply boil ½ c. balsamic vinegar for a few min. 'til thickened; stir often & watch closely.

Roasted Radicchio
and TURKEY BACON

425° Serves 4

Cuddle this next to a roast chicken or lamb ~ try it w/ Pear Salsa.

1½ Tbsp. olive oil
8 whole cloves garlic, peeled
8 shallots, peeled & halved
3 slices turkey bacon, sliced
   crosswise in thin strips
salt & pepper to taste

2 med. heads radicchio, each cut
   into quarters
olive oil
salt & pepper (again!)
Balsamic Syrup (above)

Preheat oven to 425°. Put first 5 ingred. in lg. roasting pan & stir well. Roast 15 min. Meanwhile, brush radicchio wedges liberally w/ olive oil; s & p. Stir veg. in pan, add radicchio. Roast 10 min. Carefully turn radicchio over & roast 10 min. more. Put radicchio on platter, surround w/ veg; spoon bacon over top; drizzle w/ Balsamic Syrup & serve.

Pear Salsa

Makes 3 c. +

2 c. unpeeled, chopped pears, all colors
½ c. minced yellow bell pepper
½ c. minced red onion

¼ c. chopped cilantro
¼ tsp. crushed red pepper
3 Tbsp. pear or orange juice

Mix all ingred. together & refrigerate 1 hr. to "marry" flavors.

Chopped Brussels Sprouts

(COOK 'TIL TENDER)

Trim 5-6 Brussels sprouts per person & drop into boiling water. Drain, chop fine. Stir w/ butter, minced parsley, s & p. (Make ahead to here, reheat in 350° oven.) Drizzle w/ Balsamic Syrup (above); sprinkle w/ Parmesan & serve.

Curried Pumpkin Pots

450° Serves 10

You can make these ahead; not only are they delicious, they make the table look darling.

2½ lbs. butternut squash, peeled, cut into ½" slices

1 lg. leek, cleaned, most of green removed, halved

3 green apples, peeled, cored & halved

olive oil spray

10 miniature pumpkins "JACK BE LITTLE"

½ tsp. curry ⎫ mix
½ c. butter ⎭ together

2 Tbsp. heavy cream

2 Tbsp. butter

1 tsp. curry

Preheat oven to 450°. Prepare squash, leeks & apples; spray baking sheet w/ olive oil & lay out veg. Spray lightly & roast 30 min. Meanwhile, cut off tops of pumpkins, scrape them out cleanly, clean lids too; rub insides w/ curry-butter mixture & set aside. Place all roasted veg. in food processor; add cream, butter & curry; process 'til smooth. Season w/ s & p. Fill each pumpkin, replace lids & set aside 'til ready to bake. Bake at 400° for 30 min. (longer if they're cold) 'til pumpkins feel tender when lightly squeezed. Serve.

THE MOON CAME UP, YELLOW AS A PRAIRIE COWSLIP.

♡ Bess Streeter Aldrich

STUFFED PORTABELLO MUSHROOMS

400° Serves 6

Interesting side dish ~ make ahead & cook when ready.

1 c. (packed) fresh basil leaves
1/3 c. grated Parmesan
1 Tbsp. goat cheese (or soft butter)
1 clove garlic — put through garlic press
1/4 tsp. salt
1/8 tsp. cayenne
1/3 c. olive oil
12 Portabello mushrooms (2"-3" across)
4-5 lg. fresh basil leaves, chopped
1 1/2 c. shredded mozzarella

Preheat oven to 400°. Put 1st 7 ingred. in blender & blend well. Wipe mushrooms clean w/ p. towels, carefully remove stems & put mushrooms stem side up on foil lined baking sheet. Divide basil mixture between mushrooms — spread evenly over gills to edges. Sprinkle on fresh basil; divide mozzarella between mushrooms. Cook 8-10 min.

MUM'S THE WORD

My favorite word is "PUMPKIN."

You are a pumpkin. Or you are not. I am.

Harrison Salisbury

PARMESAN SPAGHETTI SQUASH

350° Serves 4

Makes a lovely little nest for salmon (p. 80) or lamb (p. 76), among other things.

1-4 lb. spaghetti squash
2 Tbsp. butter
1/2 c. raisins (opt.)
1/4 c. chopped pistachio nuts (opt.)
3/4 c. grated Parmesan
salt & freshly ground pepper

Preheat oven to 350°. Pierce squash deeply w/ knife. Put on baking sheet & into oven for 1 hr. (turn it after 1/2 hr.). Remove from oven & cool to touch. Cut in half lengthwise; remove strings & seeds (I use shears to help it along). Drag fork through squash to make "spaghetti" & place in bowl in fridge. When ready to serve, melt butter in lg. skillet, add squash, raisins & nuts. Heat through, remove from heat; toss w/ Parmesan, salt & pepper. (So versatile; try it w/ tomato sauce; or mix in sliced sausages)

Wild Mushroom Ragout

450°   6 Servings

Serve this rustic fall dish in an oval copper pan or heavy pottery casserole. Delicious on salad greens, over garlic bread, on top of steaks & chicken, over pasta, or on pizza.

3 lbs. mixed fresh mushrooms
3 oz. mixed dried mushrooms
¼ c. olive oil
3 Tbsp. minced shallots
6 cloves garlic, crushed
¼ c. chicken broth
2 Tbsp. cognac

2 Tbsp. butter
salt & pepper
2-4" sprigs rosemary
2-4" sprigs thyme

Garnish

¼ c. chopped flat-leaf parsley
more fresh sprigs of rosemary & thyme
Parmesan curls

Preheat oven to 450°. Prepare fresh mushrooms: Wipe or brush away any dirt—do not wash; remove stems. Quarter or slice mushrooms ¼" thick. Leave little ones whole. Pour boiling water over dried mushrooms & soak 10 min. 'til tender; rinse well & dry. To a large, very hot, dry skillet add olive oil & fresh mushrooms; stir often over high heat. When mushrooms begin to release juices add shallots, garlic & rehydrated mushrooms. Cook until liquid begins to evaporate; stir in broth, cognac & butter. Season w/ s & p, add herbs, stir well, pour into casserole; roast, uncovered, 30 min.; stir occasionally. Remove from oven, discard herb stems, stir in fresh herbs (leave herb sprigs whole); use potato peeler or sharp knife to make Parmesan curls. Serve.

It's BEIGE! MY COLOR! *Elsie de Wolf*

Corn Pudding

350° Serves 8–10

Serve this with heated maple syrup to everyone when they come back from trick-or-treating or take it to a harvest potluck — moist inside, with a nice crisp edge — a guaranteed crowd-pleaser.

1 c. sour cream
1-14 oz. can corn, drained
1-14 oz. can creamed corn
½ c. butter, melted

1 egg, beaten
1 box Jiffy corn-muffin-mix
¼ tsp. cayenne
¼ tsp. paprika

(opt.: heated maple syrup)

Preheat oven to 350°. Mix first 7 ingred. & pour into buttered 9" square baking dish. Sprinkle top w/paprika; bake 1 hr. Heat maple syrup, if desired, & serve pudding hot or warm. Oh! p.s. — it's great for brunch too!

Mari-Gold-Dust:

Fresh marigold petals are wonderful in salads, chowder, rice, muffins. To make "dust" for winter use: wash flower heads, pick off petals, remove white "heel". Dry in 150°-200° oven for 2 hrs. Crumble into shaker jar.

54

Indiana Ham and Sweet Potato Soup

375° Serves 8

Just spicy enough to make it interesting ~ pop the veg. into the oven early in the day & this goes together in a flash.

2 med. lg. (about 1½ lbs.) sweet
   potatoes; washed, dried & pierced
6 (about ¾ lbs.) carrots; topped, tailed
   & peeled
1 lg. onion, peeled & quartered
1 lg. clove garlic, skin on
1½ lbs. smoked ham hocks
8 c. water
1 lb. yellow split peas, rinsed
1 Tbsp. butter

1½ tsp. rubbed (or ground) sage
1 Tbsp. Cholula (Mexican hot sauce)
¼ tsp. cayenne
1 tsp. salt
½ tsp. freshly ground pepper
¼ c. heavy cream
1 c. diced ham steak
Zest from 1 lg. orange
½ c. minced parsley
1 can potato sticks (opt.)

Preheat oven to 375°. Place 1st 4 ingred. in lightly oiled roasting pan & into oven. Cook 1½ hrs.~ turn all after 1 hr. Remove, split open potatoes, cool to touch. Remove garlic from skin. Meanwhile, put ham hocks & water in lg. soup pot. Bring to boil (skim off any foam); simmer 1 hr.; add split peas, simmer 45 min. more, all w/ lid slightly askew. Remove ham hocks from soup; when cool enough, remove meat from ham hocks, dice & put back into pot. Put roasted veg. into food processor; add butter & next 5 ingred. Process well. Add cream, process & stir all into soup pot. Stir in diced ham & zest; simmer. Serve, sprinkled w/ parsley ~ & pass a bowl of potato sticks for garnish (if you like).

Chicken Stock 101

Dark brown & rich, the perfect base for wonderful fall soups & gravies. Toss cheese tortellini into hot broth with chopped broccoli, s & p, and shredded Parmesan. Or caramelize some onions & roast some carrots; add them to broth w/ chicken meat ~ sprinkle over lemon thyme. Add canned tomatoes, garlic & lots of veggies, & either rice, barley, beans or noodles. A grated potato will thicken soup. For biscuits & gravy, boil stock down, thicken w/ arrowroot or flour; put hot chicken on top of split biscuits & pour gravy over.

1 chicken w/ giblets (big)
2 Tbsp. olive oil
2 lg. onions, unpeeled
2-3 carrots, unpeeled
2-3 celery ribs, w/ leaves
1 tsp. whole peppercorns
2 bay leaves
handful of fresh parsley

Wash chicken, discard liver & roughly chop heart, gizzard & neck; add to hot oil in deep soup pot. Over high heat, cook, stirring occasionally. Quarter onion & add to pot. Continue cooking 'til chicken is VERY brown, but not burnt. Add in 1 c. water, stir & scrape all brown bits from bottom of pot (deglaze). Roughly chop remaining veggies & add to pot. Add rest of ingred. including whole chicken & water to cover. Bring to boil, skim off any foam, set lid askew & reduce heat to simmer. Chicken will be done in about 1 hr. Remove it from pot, cool to touch. Remove meat to fridge; put skin & bones back into pot. Continue simmering 4-5 hours, adding more water when needed. Cool a bit before straining into lg. bowl; put uncovered stock in fridge overnight. The fat will rise to the top & harden & you can easily lift it off. Underneath will be vitamin-rich, delicious broth. Stretch it by adding water or canned broth. Freeze in ice-cube trays for "insta-sauce."

French Chicken Soup

425° Serves 8

We have a little farm in California, where I am right now, writing this page; it's all fruit trees & hummingbirds. ♥ Fall lasts a lot longer here than it does on the Vineyard ~ pretty much all winter! Yesterday friends came for lunch; it was a blustery day w/ leaves flying. I made salad from the garden & set a table under the apple tree & served this tummy-warming soup in charming little ovenproof soup pots I found in a local second-hand store. YUM!

8 c. chicken stock (p. 56)
2 lbs. fresh mushrooms
(½ baby bells, ½ shitake)
3 Tbsp. butter
4 Tbsp. olive oil
6 onions, thinly sliced
2 cloves garlic, pressed
¼ c. flour

1 Tbsp. Dijon mustard
1 Tbsp. dried thyme
1 tsp. black pepper
½ c. white port
¼ c. tomato puree
½ c. fresh minced parsley
salt to taste
3-4 c. cooked chicken
4 c. Gruyère cheese, grated

Make chicken stock the day before you want to serve this soup, or even a few days before. Slice & cook mushrooms in 1 Tbsp. olive oil in a large skillet until soft; set aside. In the same pan, melt butter, 3 Tbsp. oil; over med. heat, cook onions for 30-40 min., stirring often until golden brown. Add garlic, stir well & cook another 2 min. Sprinkle flour over, stir well, cook another 2 min. Pour 1 c. stock into pan, stir well, scraping up brown bits from bottom, then pour all into lg. soup pot & add the rest of stock. Stir in mustard, thyme & pepper; boil 5 min. Preheat oven to 425°. Add port & tomato puree to pot; simmer 20 min. Stir in parsley & salt to taste. Into each ovenproof soup bowl, put about ½ c. chunks of chicken meat; divide mushrooms evenly between bowls; fill each w/ broth; top each w/ about ½ c. cheese. Bake (uncovered) 'til brown on top, about 20 min. Serve.

IF I DIDN'T START PAINTING, I WOULD HAVE RAISED CHICKENS. ♥ Grandma Moses

He heard sound coming. Rain like hundreds of mice running through corn.

VIRGINIA HAMILTON

TOMATO SOUP

Serves 4

1 Tbsp. olive oil
2 cloves garlic, pressed
1-28 oz. can crushed tomatoes
   in puree (organic, if possible)
½ c. chicken broth
1 Tbsp. butter

1 Tbsp. lemon juice
½ tsp. salt
¼ tsp. pepper
2 Tbsp. minced fresh basil
   or parsley
shredded Parmesan cheese

Heat oil in med. saucepan. Sizzle garlic, add tomatoes & all other ingred. except Parmesan, simmer 10 min. Serve, sprinkled w/ Parmesan. Optional: 10 oz. cooked cheese tortellini, cooked & crumbled sausage, diced tofu, or shrimp.

I've never known anyone yet who doesn't suffer a certain restlessness when autumn rolls around.... we're all eight years old again & anything is possible.
— Sue Grafton

RAINY SATURDAY LUNCH
Menu

GRILLED CHEESE SANDWICH
TOMATO SOUP
BROWNIE (P. 107)
COLD MILK
YOUR BOOK-OF-THE-MOMENT AND/OR A
SHIRLEY TEMPLE or ROY ROGERS MOVIE.

Neat as a freshly peeled
Easter egg,
just six years old, he sat,
come what may, outside the door of Room 2.
after Else Lasker-Schüler

THERE'S A BACK-TO-SCHOOL FEELING IN THE AIR....

LANGUAGE
MATH
CREATIVE WRITING
HISTORY

8343883 TICKET TO SUCCESS 8343883

MANNERS
ART
N A T U R E
OUR WORLD
Science

WHAT ONE LOVES IN CHILDHOOD STAYS IN THE HEART FOREVER

LET US PUT OUR MINDS
TOGETHER AND
SEE WHAT KIND OF
LIFE WE CAN MAKE
FOR OUR CHILDREN.
Sitting Bull

AND YOU WROTE ON MY SLATE "I LOVE YOU SO," WHEN WE WERE A COUPLE OF KIDS.

READIN' & WRITIN' & 'RITHMETIC, TAUGHT TO THE TUNE OF THE HICKORY STICK,

YOU WERE MY QUEEN OF CALICO, I WAS YOUR BASHFUL BAREFOOT BEAU,

You can never go home again, but the truth is you can never leave home, so it's all right. — MAYA ANGELOU

Farmhouse Biscuits

450° Makes 12

For a heavenly Sunday supper, make a crisp, juicy roast chicken, & serve it w/ cranberry sauce & these hot biscuits split & slathered w/ Bee Butter (p.61). Everyone will love you for it!

1½ c. flour
2½ tsp. baking powder

½ tsp. baking soda
½ tsp. salt
1 c. sour cream

Preheat oven to 350°. Butter a baking sheet & flour a work surface. Combine 1st 4 ingred. Mix in sour cream with fingers just until blended. Get the mess to hold together; transfer to floured surface. Pat dough out to ½" thick. Cut dough w/ a 2" round cutter (dip it in flour). Bake 10-12 min. 'til lightly browned.

HOT TURKEY SANDWICH

PILE LEFTOVER TURKEY ON SPLIT & BUTTERED BISCUITS.

POUR OVER GRAVY; S & P; mmmmmm.

& The animals talk in reasonable tones that children understand. — Maxine Kumin

60

Iowa Corn Bread

With Bee Butter

400° SERVES 8-10

CRUSTY ON THE OUTSIDE, TENDER ON THE INSIDE.

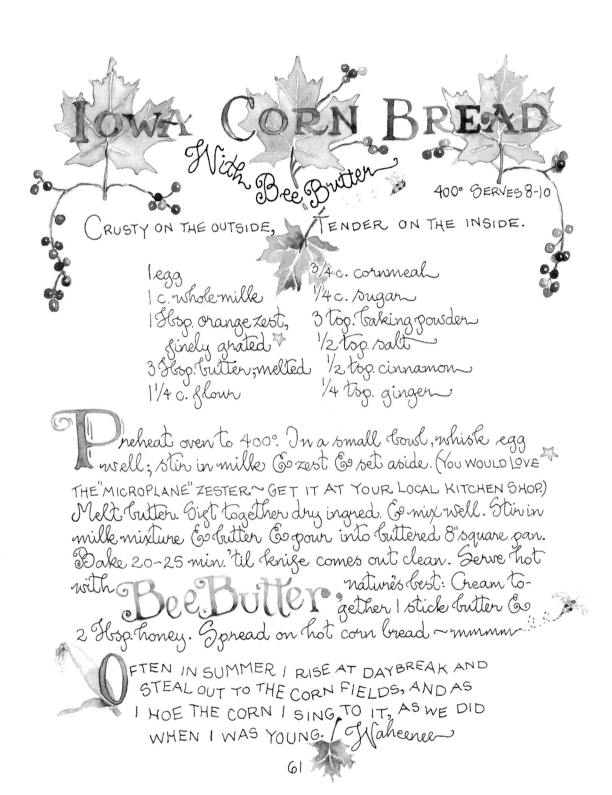

1 egg
1 c. whole milk
1 tbsp. orange zest, finely grated
3 tbsp. butter, melted
1¼ c. flour

¾ c. cornmeal
¼ c. sugar
3 tsp. baking powder
½ tsp. salt
½ tsp. cinnamon
¼ tsp. ginger

Preheat oven to 400°. In a small bowl, whisk egg well; stir in milk & zest & set aside. (YOU WOULD LOVE THE "MICROPLANE" ZESTER ~ GET IT AT YOUR LOCAL KITCHEN SHOP.) Melt butter. Sift together dry ingred. & mix well. Stir in milk mixture & butter & pour into buttered 8" square pan. Bake 20-25 min. 'til knife comes out clean. Serve hot with **Bee Butter**, nature's best: Cream together 1 stick butter & 2 tbsp. honey. Spread on hot corn bread ~ mmmm

OFTEN IN SUMMER I RISE AT DAYBREAK AND STEAL OUT TO THE CORN FIELDS, AND AS I HOE THE CORN I SING TO IT, AS WE DID WHEN I WAS YOUNG. Waheenee

THANKSGIVING

On a crisp fall day when I am out walking in the COLOR-splashed woods, leaves blowing on the wind, cicadas singing & geese winging their way south — the leaf-crunch my boots make is the only "people" sound I hear. Being in the woods is like a time warp, they're as primitive now as they ever were. With no signs of "progress" around, it's easy to step back in time. I can feel Indians around me, almost see them going through the trees; it's so quiet, I imagine I hear their horses & smell their campfires. I'm in a nature-trance & it's 1620 in New England.

What would an Autumn book (inspired by nature) BE without a deep bow to the heart, poetry & legend of the Native American? And WHAT would Thanksgiving be without them——?

I love to read Indian orations. They're so beautiful-touching & simple & straight from the heart.

And when your children's children think themselves alone in the silence of the pathless woods, they will not be alone. At night when the streets of your cities and villages are silent, and you think them deserted, they will throng with the returning hosts that once filled them and still love this beautiful land. You will never be alone.

CHIEF SEATTLE

HEAP HIGH THE BOARD WITH PLENTEOUS CHEER, & GATHER TO THE FEAST, & TOAST THE STURDY PILGRIM BAND WHOSE COURAGE NEVER CEASED. — ALICE WILLIAMS BROTHERTON

The first Thanksgiving took place outdoors in the Autumn of 1621. It was a huge 3-day event; along with the 51 pilgrims who had survived after landing at Plymouth the previous March, there were 90 Wampanoag Indians who had helped the colonists get settled. The Indians brought 5 deer to the celebration & along with the venison, they all feasted on roast duck, roast goose, wild turkey, corn bread, squash, berries, maple sugar, wild plums & pumpkins. Sound familiar?

Here's our version last year. We put the table in a field under tall trees next to a creek. While we ate, leaves came down; we had family and friends, the dogs, the cats & even Sky, my sister's horse, hung his head over the fence for his apple treats. For dessert, we had a bonfire! The basic Thanksgiving menu hasn't changed much, but every family has its own traditional holiday favorites. Here are a few of our Thanksgiving MUST-HAVES ~ They just give us more to be thankful for.

No more turkey, but I'd like another serving of that bread he ate. anon.

My Grandma's Stuffing

AND HER MOM'S, & MY MOM'S & MINE...

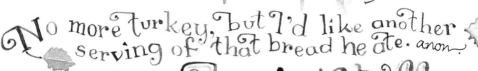

Very old-fashioned, very original ~ I've never seen this method in any cookbooks ~ but our Thanksgiving CENTERS around the flavoring & tasting of this delicious stuffing. ♥

3 giant loaves cheap, soft bread, 2 white, 1 brown
1 c. butter
3 med. onions, chopped
6 stalks celery, "

1 jar sage leaves, about ½ c.
1 tbsp. salt, or to taste
freshly ground pepper
optional: sausage, apples, nuts, prunes, oysters, etc., BUT WE LIKE IT PLAIN.

Three days before Turkey Day, spread the bread on cookie sheets to dry naturally. Fill your clean kitchen sink w/ 6" of the hottest water you can stand to touch. Dip each slice of bread in water & wring out well. Put it into a large bowl, breaking it up a bit as you go ~ it should be chunky, doughy, chewy. Melt butter in a lg. skillet; slowly sauté onions & celery. Meanwhile, over the sink, rub sage leaves between your palms, discard woody stems & put sage in w/ bread. Pour butter mixture over bread & mix well w/ your hands (but don't burn yourself!). Stir in opt. ingred. if desired. Add salt ~ it needs to be a LITTLE bit salty (the turkey will absorb it) ~ then pepper. Now for the tasting, everyone has an opinion! More salt? More sage? More butter? Don't worry, this recipe is no-fail! Loosely stuff turkey & bake any left over in a separate dish.

64

SWEET POTATO
Casserole

350° Serves 8

For a total Thanksgiving showstopper, fill miniature pumpkins w/ this mixture (see p. 51); put the turkey on a huge tray & surround it w/ pumpkins. Otherwise a heavy casserole will do just fine. Just make sure these potatoes are on the table!

4 c. sweet potatoes, cooked & mashed
8 oz. cream cheese, softened
½ c. butter, softened
2 eggs, beaten

¼ c. brown sugar
2½ tbsp. dry sherry
¼ tsp. salt
¾ c. chopped walnuts
½ tsp. nutmeg

THANKSGIVING GREETING

Thankful be all
hearts and gay
Within your home
Thanksgiving Day

Joe collects
postcards –
me, too,
but I collect
mine
from Joe!

Preheat oven to 350°. With electric mixer (not food processor), whip all ingred. except walnuts & nutmeg, until light. Stir in walnuts & put into a buttered casserole. Spread evenly & sprinkle nutmeg over the top. Bake 45 min. 'til golden.

A Thanksgiving Blessing

A HOUSE NEEDS A GRANDMA IN IT. ♥ *Louisa May Alcott*

My grandma was our main holiday tradition. She was always there, smelling like onion, sage & cookie dough. She wore an apron while she cooked, & pulled us aside to give surprise gifts, making each of us feel like the most important grandchild in the world.

Nothing on earth can make up for the loss of one who has loved you. ♥ *Selma Lagerlöf*

TOUCH HANDS, TOUCH HANDS
WITH THOSE THAT STAY...
WM. H.H. MURRAY

Florence Orr Smith
1909 ~ 2001

O, thou who has given

WE DO NOT REMEMBER DAYS, WE REMEMBER MOMENTS. CESARE PAVESE

RAINBOW JELL-O
SERVES 12 OR MORE

The LIGHT came on in my 2-yr.-old nephew's little face last Thanksgiving when the Jell-O came out — "YELLO!" he exclaimed, & his day was MADE. Wonderful for little people, but big people love it too.

1 - 6 oz. pkg. orange Jell-O
1   "   lemon   "
1   "   lime   "
1   "   cherry   "
4 c. (2 pints) sour cream

You need a straight-sided glass bowl for this so you can see all the beautiful colors. Start with orange Jell-O: dissolve it in 2 c. boiling water. To ½ c. of the liquid, add 1 c. sour cream & stir well. Pour this mixture into bowl & put into fridge to chill. When set, gently pour over the rest of the orange Jell-O & chill until firm. Repeat w/ remaining colors in order given. (p.s. this is a side dish,   not a dessert ♥.)

a grateful heart. ♥ George Herbert

us so much; mercifully grant

us one   thing more

67

GRAVY

ONE OF THE LUCKIEST THINGS THAT CAN HAPPEN TO YOU IN LIFE IS TO HAVE A HAPPY CHILDHOOD.
— Agatha Christie

In our family, gravy is the Holy Grail of Thanksgiving. ♥ And nothing could be worse than not having enough! Now I have a

SECRET WEAPON.

A couple of days before Thanksgiving I make extra gravy. Here's how: Follow the recipe for Chicken Stock (p. 56), but use turkey wings, legs & giblets instead of chicken (if you can't find turkey giblets, chicken is OK). When the stock is done, boil it down a little to make it especially rich & flavorful; keep in fridge 'til TURKEY DAY, then: Remove the neck & giblets from the turkey (by the way, every basic cookbook has a recipe for roast turkey, including my Christmas book, which is why I'm using the space in this book for other things!). Anyway, chop the neck & giblets in big pieces (no liver!) & brown them well in 1 Tbsp. olive oil in a lg. saucepan over med. high heat. Pour in 1 c. water & scrape up brown bits stuck to bottom of pan. Add 1 roughly chopped onion, 1 chopped carrot, 1 chopped celery stalk (w/ leaves), 3 parsley sprigs, 1 bay leaf & 8 peppercorns; add water to cover. Simmer, w/ lid set askew 'til turkey comes out of oven (add more water if it gets too low); strain it. Remove turkey from roasting pan, cover it & set aside to "rest." Set roaster w/ juices over med. high heat, bring to boil, then pour in strained broth & scrape up all brown bits from roaster. Either spoon fat off top, or put juices in wide flat dish & into freezer to allow fat to come to top; scrape off & discard. Put the juices in a lg. saucepan, reheat & bring out the SECRET WEAPON, add it to the pan, bring to boil. Taste for strength, boil down if necessary. In a shaker jar combine ½ c. water & 6 Tbsp. flour & shake well. Slowly, whisking constantly, add just enough flour-mix to thicken the gravy to your liking. Season well w/ s & p. I serve gravy in a small pitcher ~ easiest for little hands to pass ♥.

HEIRLOOMS WE DON'T HAVE IN OUR FAMILY, BUT STORIES WE'VE GOT.
♥ Rose Chernin

WE RUN EVERYTHING BY THE BIG DADDY

TASTE MASTER GUY

Cranberry Sauce

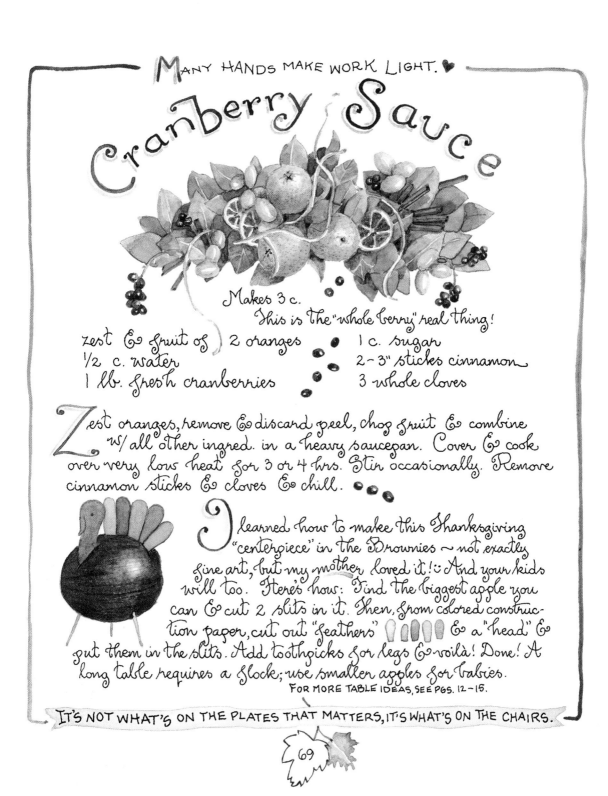

Makes 3 c.

This is the "whole berry" real thing!

zest & fruit of) 2 oranges   1 c. sugar
½ c. water   2 – 3" sticks cinnamon
1 lb. fresh cranberries   3 whole cloves

Zest oranges, remove & discard peel, chop fruit & combine
w/ all other ingred. in a heavy saucepan. Cover & cook
over very low heat for 3 or 4 hrs. Stir occasionally. Remove
cinnamon sticks & cloves & chill. ●●●

I learned how to make this Thanksgiving
"centerpiece" in the Brownies ~ not exactly
fine art, but my mother loved it! ☺ And your kids
will too. Here's how: Find the biggest apple you
can & cut 2 slits in it. Then, from colored construc-
tion paper, cut out "feathers" & a "head" &
put them in the slits. Add toothpicks for legs & voilà! Done! A
long table requires a flock; use smaller apples for babies.

FOR MORE TABLE IDEAS, SEE PGS. 12 – 15.

IT'S NOT WHAT'S ON THE PLATES THAT MATTERS, IT'S WHAT'S ON THE CHAIRS.

COUNTING OUR BLESSINGS

A PRAYER FOR A LITTLE HOME

God send us a little home; To come back to when we roam.

One picture on each wall; not many things at all.

Wooden floors & fluted tiles; wide windows, a view for miles.

God send us a little ground; Tall trees stand 'round.

Red finelight & deep chairs; Small white beds upstairs.

Homely flowers in fertile sod; Overhead, thy stars, O God.

Great talk in little nooks; soft colors, rows of books.

God bless thee when winds blow; Our home & all we know.

Florence Bone

MAIN DISHES

Spring shall plant
and Autumn garner
until the end of time.
♥ Robert Browning

71

Scallops, Mashed Potatoes, AND Corn Chowder

SERVES 6

Everything in this bacon-spiced, tummy-warming, one-dish dinner can be made ahead & reheated. Serve it in wide, shallow bowls w/ a big spoon & a fork.

Corn Chowder

8 strips bacon, thickly sliced
1 lg. yellow onion, finely chopped
2 stalks celery, chopped
2 c. fresh corn (cut off the cob)
   (frozen corn is OK too)
2 lg. carrots, 1/2" slices
1-14 oz. can creamed corn
3 c. milk
1/3 c. heavy cream

1/4 to 1/2 tsp. red pepper
   flakes (to taste)
1/4 tsp. ground sage
3 Tbsp. chopped chives SAVE FOR GARNISH

BUTTERMILK MASHED POTATOES
1/2 RECIPE, P.49

Scallops

2 lbs. sea scallops (3 or 4 per serving)
1/4 c. canola oil
salt & pepper

In a large, heavy saucepan, slowly cook bacon until VERY crisp; drain on paper towels; cut w/scissors into 1" pieces & set aside.

Pour off all but 1 Tbsp. bacon fat. Put onion & celery into bacon fat & cook over med. heat 'til softened ~about 10 min.

NEXT PAGE PLEASE →

72

Stir in corn, carrots, creamed corn & milk. Simmer gently for about 25 min., stirring occasionally, until carrots are tender. (Meanwhile make ½ of the recipe for Buttermilk Mashed Potatoes on p. 49) To milk & corn mixture add cream, red pepper flakes, sage & half the reserved bacon pieces. Stir & keep warm while you make the

Scallops.
Rinse off scallops & dry well. Heat oil in lg. skillet to med. hot. In batches (do not crowd or you won't get color), sauté scallops 1½ min. each side 'til very golden. (If overcooked, they will be tough & dry.) Salt & pepper them.

TO SERVE

Put a scoop of mashed potatoes in the center of each shallow bowl & ladle chowder around potatoes. Top each w/ 3 or 4 scallops & garnish each dish w/reserved bacon & chives. Salt & pepper to taste.

Delicious autumn!
My very soul is
wedded to it, and if I were a
bird I would fly about the
earth seeking the
successive autumns.
George Eliot

Chicken in Cream Sauce over Happy Rice

Serves 4 to 6

Just yummy. Hide any leftovers so you can have them all to yourself for hot lunch tomorrow. Roasted carrots or plain string beans are both good w/ this.

2 lbs. skinless, boneless chicken thighs and/or breasts
1 Tbsp. dried thyme
1/4 tsp. cayenne
salt & pepper to taste
4 Tbsp. butter
3 c. sliced mushrooms

1/3 c. minced shallots
1 1/4 c. chicken broth
1 c. dry white wine
1 c. heavy cream
1/3 c. chopped parsley
HAPPY RICE (below)
3 red pears, diced

Wash & cut chicken into 1" pieces; sprinkle them w/ thyme, cayenne, salt & pepper. Melt 2 Tbsp. butter in lg. skillet; cook chicken over med.-high heat for 3 min. ~ do not overcook. Add in mushrooms & cook 2 min. more. Remove chicken & mushrooms from skillet & set aside. Melt remaining 2 Tbsp. butter; cook shallots for 2 min., stir often. Add broth & wine to pan; bring to boil, scraping up brown bits from bottom of pan. Simmer 5 min.; add cream; simmer 5 min. more. Put chicken & mushrooms back into skillet, add parsley & heat through. Spoon chicken over rice. Sprinkle chopped pears over all & serve.

HAPPY RICE

Makes 6 servings (5 c.)

1 1/2 c. uncooked white rice
1/2 c. sliced almonds

1/3 c. golden raisins, chopped
seeds from 1 lg. pomegranate (opt.)

Cook rice according to pkg. instructions. When done, stir in all additional ingredients. NOTE: You can make Happy Rice even HAPPIER (when serving it in a menu that has no sauce) by adding 1/2 stick butter, 1/2 c. minced green onion, 1 Tbsp. minced fresh thyme, 2 tsp. orange zest, salt, pepper & 2 diced red pears.

One-Dish
Stuffed Pork Chops,
Sweet Potatoes and Apples

400° 6 SERVINGS

4 lg. sweet potatoes
2 Tbsp. canola oil
6-2" thick pork chops
salt & pepper

Stuffing (recipe below)
8 lg. green apples
1 c. golden raisins
1 tsp. cinnamon

Preheat oven to 400°. Peel potatoes, halve them, & boil them 'til about half - done. Set aside. Heat oil in lg. skillet & brown chops on both sides ~ salt & pepper. Remove from pan & cool. Make stuffing. Cut a deep slit in the side of each chop & fill w/stuffing. Put chops & potatoes into lg. baking pan. Peel, halve & core apples; arrange them in pan w/chops & potatoes & sprinkle on raisins. Sprinkle each apple w/cinnamon. Cover the pan tightly with foil. Bake 50 minutes & serve. ♥

Stuffing

1 stick butter
1 lg. onion, finely chopped
3 celery ribs, chopped
½ c. minced parsley
2 c. plain, dry bread crumbs
salt & pepper

Melt butter in skillet; add onion & celery & cook slowly 'til soft. Add parsley, bread crumbs, s & p. Mix well & correct consistency w/more bread crumbs or butter ♥.

IT IS THE SWEET, SIMPLE THINGS OF LIFE WHICH ARE THE REAL ONES AFTER ALL. ♥ Laura Ingalls Wilder

Braised Lamb Shanks

400° Serves 6

Easy, but that's not all: "You can sit down & visit with your guests while the smell of this delicious dish wafts through the house." From my English pen pal, the adorable Rachel Ashby.

3 c. lentils	1½ Tbsp. dried oregano
6 c. beef broth	freshly ground black pepper
3 Tbsp. brown sugar	6 lbs. lamb shanks (try for
	12 small, or 6 large)

Preheat oven to 400°. In a lg. heavy covered casserole, stir all ingred. together in order given. Cover tightly; bake 45 min., turn lambs, cook 45 min. more. Serve. (A delicious side dish: spoon this into a nest of Parmesan Spaghetti Squash, p. 52.)

Macaroni & Cheese

375° Serves 4-6

10 oz. elbow macaroni	½ tsp. salt
2 eggs	¼ tsp. pepper
1 Tbsp. dry mustard	2 c. half & half
	1 lb. sharp cheddar cheese, grated

Preheat oven to 375°. Cook & drain macaroni. In a lg. bowl, lightly beat eggs w/mustard, s & p. Stir in half & half, then cheese, then macaroni. Pour into buttered 2-qt. casserole; bake 25 min. Put under broiler 1 min. to make top brown & crisp.

COOKS, LIKE ALL MUST HAVE AN AUDIENCE GREAT ARTISTS, WORTH COOKING FOR.

Andre Simon

ORANGE SPICED

Harvest Stew

Serves 8

Best when made a day ahead, reheated & brought to the table, with autumn ganache, in a roasted pumpkin.

4 Tbsp. vegetable oil

3 lbs. beef chuck, in 1" cubes

2 med. onions, chopped

2 cloves garlic, minced

½ sm. can tomato paste

½ c. flour

3 c. beef broth

2 c. good red wine, pinot noir

3 parsnips, sliced

3 Yukon Gold potatoes, peeled & cut in ½" cubes

3 carrots, sliced

3 ribs celery, sliced

3 c. butternut squash, in ½" cubes

Bouquet garni: in a piece of cheesecloth, tie up 2 bay leaves, 4 cloves, 6 sprigs of parsley, 2-3" sprigs rosemary, 3-3" sprigs thyme, zest of 1 orange (no white pith)

1 - 10 to 12 lbs. pumpkin

Make bouquet garni & set aside. Heat 1 Tbsp. oil in lg. covered casserole or soup pot; brown beef quickly over high heat in 3 batches, adding more oil as needed; set beef aside. In same pot, over med. heat, in 1 Tbsp. oil, cook onion 'til soft. Add in garlic & tomato paste; stir & cook 2 min. Stir in flour, cook 2 min. more; then beef broth & wine; stir well, scraping bits off bottom of pot. Add in vegetables, the meat & bouquet garni. Cover, simmer over low heat 2 hrs; stirring occasionally. Taste; season w/ s & p. Cool, cover & refrigerate overnight. On the day of serving, prepare PUMPKIN: Preheat oven to 400°. Cut top off pumpkin, remove seeds & scrape inside as dry as possible. Rub outside w/ veg. oil, roast 20 min. Fill w/ hot stew, set lid askew & serve.

THE WOOD IS GLAD TO THE PERSON WHO IS USING IT,

THE WAY TO A MAN'S HEART

TOUCHDOWN CHILI

THIS IS MUY BUENO, TEXAS-STYLE; JOE BESAME MUCHO WHEN I MAKE IT. ♥ PERFECTO CON CORN BREAD. SERVES 8

3 Tbsp. canola oil
3 lbs. beef chuck, in 1" pieces
4 cloves garlic, minced
1/4 c. chili powder
1/4 c. flour
1 Tbsp. dried oregano

1 Tbsp. ground cumin
3½ c. beef broth ★
2 - 15 oz. cans pinto beans, drained & rinsed well
opt. garnishes: chopped red onion, sour cream, cilantro

★ Homemade or canned broth are both fine, but I use a product called "Better Than Bouillon," available in the soup aisle of supermarkets in chicken or beef flavors. IT'S GOOD!

In a lg. heavy pot, heat oil & brown beef chunks in 3 batches. When last batch is almost done, add garlic & cook 3 min. more. Put all the beef back into pot; stir in chili, flour, oregano & cumin. Slowly stir in 2½ c. beef broth. Stir well, cover & simmer 1½ hrs. Stir occasionally; take care not to scorch bottom. Over time, stir in remaining 1 c. beef broth. At the end of the cooking time add in beans, stir well & serve.

No COMPOSER HAS YET CAUGHT THIS RHYTHM OF AMERICA— IT IS TOO MIGHTY FOR THE EARS OF MOST. ♥ ISADORA DUNCAN

Turkey in the Straw

Serves 2

Crunchy & delicious, almost no carbs, our favorite fast & healthy dinner. Great way to use up leftover turkey.

2 Tbsp. olive oil
2 tsp. toasted sesame oil
2 tsp. chili garlic sauce
   (in Asian food aisle)
2 c. sliced mushrooms
1 lg. clove garlic, minced
1 12-oz. pkg. broccoli slaw

2 c. cooked turkey in bite-sized
   pieces, or cooked chicken,
   shrimp or salmon chunks
salt & pepper
2 Tbsp. chopped dry-roasted
   peanuts or chopped walnuts
shredded Parmesan, to taste

Combine first 3 ingred. in a lg. skillet over med. high heat. Add mushrooms; cook 'til soft. Stir in garlic & cook 1 min. more. Add broccoli slaw; cook & stir 'til slightly wilted. Stir in turkey, s & p to taste. Heat through (but don't overcook broccoli), divide onto 2 plates, sprinkle w/nuts & Parmesan cheese & serve.

FOREVER YOUNG

A few years ago, on my birthday, I was riding my exercise bike when the phone rang. It was my 87-year-old Grandma calling to wish me a happy birthday. "Is this my oldest grandchild?" she asked with a little laugh in her voice. "What are you doing?" I answered, "Riding my bike, trying to stay young (HUFF-PUFF)." There was a little pause & then she very slowly & sweetly said, "Well OK, but it won't work."

Lime Salmon
WITH LEEK FRISÉE
Serves Six

1 12-oz. can frozen limeade
¼ c. lite soy sauce
2 Tbsp. toasted sesame oil
2 tsp. chili garlic sauce (in Asian section of market)
¼ c. + 2 Tbsp. grated ginger

¼ c. chopped chives
1 tsp. lime zest
3 lb. fresh salmon, skin removed
4 leeks
3 c. canola oil

IN A MED. SAUCEPAN:

mix together 1st 7 ingred. Wash & dry salmon, cut into 6 pieces, put it in a shallow dish & pour half of lime sauce over. Reserve remaining sauce. Set salmon aside for 1 hr. Meanwhile, make the Leek Frisée: Cut off & discard green part of leeks & cut them partially down the center. Soak for 10 min., swish & drain, & rinse again. Dry well. Cut them in half & julienne into very fine pieces ⅛" × 2½". Blot dry. Drop leeks into cold oil & over med. heat bring to gentle simmer ~ cook 20 min. 'til golden. Drain on paper towels, salt to taste; reserve at room temp. Discard marinade around salmon & wipe off excess (as it burns easily); gently sauté salmon in lightly oiled pan until done. Heat up reserved lime sauce. Put filets on plates, pour sauce over & top each w/ a handful of leeks. Serve.

JUST BECAUSE YOU HAVE
FOUR CHAIRS, SIX PLATES,

AND THREE CUPS IS NO REASON
WHY YOU CAN'T INVITE TWELVE
TO DINNER. Alice May Brock

Sesame Ginger Shrimp

350° Serves 6

1- 4 to 5 lb. spaghetti squash

3 lbs. lg. shrimp, peeled, cleaned, remove tails; butterfly by cutting PARTIALLY → through each shrimp lengthwise

3/4 c. dry white wine

3/4 c. pear nectar

2 Tbsp. soy sauce

1 Tbsp. cornstarch

1 tsp. ground ginger

1/2 tsp. salt

1/4 c. + 1 Tbsp. peanut oil

10 green onions, chopped (with green part)

2 Tbsp. minced fresh ginger

2 lg. cloves garlic, put through garlic press

1 tsp. crushed red pepper flakes

1- 8 oz. can water chestnuts, rinsed & drained

zest of 1 lime

2 tsp. black sesame seeds

1/4 c. fresh basil, chopped

Preheat oven to 350°. Pierce squash deeply, put on baking sheet & into oven for 1 hr. ~ or 'til soft when pressed. Remove from oven, cut in half, remove seeds & strings (scissors help!), run fork through to make "spaghetti." You can do this ahead & reheat in microwave if you like.

Wash & prepare raw shrimp; drain. In a lg. bowl, whisk together next 6 ingred. Add shrimp to bowl, mix well, marinate 1/2 hr. Meanwhile, measure out all other ingred. Heat oil in lg. wok or skillet over high heat. Drain shrimp; reserve marinade. Stir-fry shrimp in hot oil for 1 min. (BE CAREFUL DURING THE COOKING PROCESS NOT TO OVERCOOK THE SHRIMP, YOU CAN ALWAYS COOK THEM A LITTLE MORE AT THE END.) Add in onions, ginger, garlic & red pepper flakes; cook & stir 1 min. Whisk reserved marinade & add it to pan along w/ water chestnuts & lime zest. Stir well & cook 'til sauce simmers & shrimp are done; remove from heat & stir in sesame seeds. Make a nest from spaghetti squash strands (either on individual plates or on a lg. platter) & fill w/ shrimp & sauce; sprinkle w/ basil & serve.

Potato Bugs

350° Serves 2

This is what often happens to food if you have brothers! My brother Steve made this up & it is ABSOLUTELY DELICIOUS!

1 lg. potato, scrubbed & dried
softened butter & salt
12 med. shrimp, shells &
   tails off, deveined
1½ oz. cream cheese, softened
2 Tbsp. hot milk
2 tsp. butter (melted in milk)
1 Tbsp. minced green onion
1 Tbsp. minced parsley
s & p to taste

2 Tbsp. butter
1 minced garlic clove
¼ c. grated cheddar cheese
2 black olives (opt.!)

Preheat oven to 350°. Smear potato w/ softened butter, salt it & bake for 1 to 1¼ hrs. 'til done. Meantime, clean shrimp & set aside. Grate the cheddar cheese. When potato is done, cool to handle. Cut in half lengthwise & carefully remove cooked potato to bowl, reserving skin whole. Mash potato w/ cream cheese, milk & butter, onion & parsley. S & p to taste. Melt 2 Tbsp. butter w/ garlic & drench the raw shrimp in it. Hang shrimp over potato skin (as pictured above), fill skin w/ potato mixture, sprinkle over grated cheese & bake 15 min. more. Remove from oven, add olive slices for "eyes" & serve.

my brotha STEPHEN STEWART

if i cud ever write a poem as beautiful
   as u, little 2/yr/old/ brotha,
poetry wud go out of bizness.
     SONIA SANCHEZ

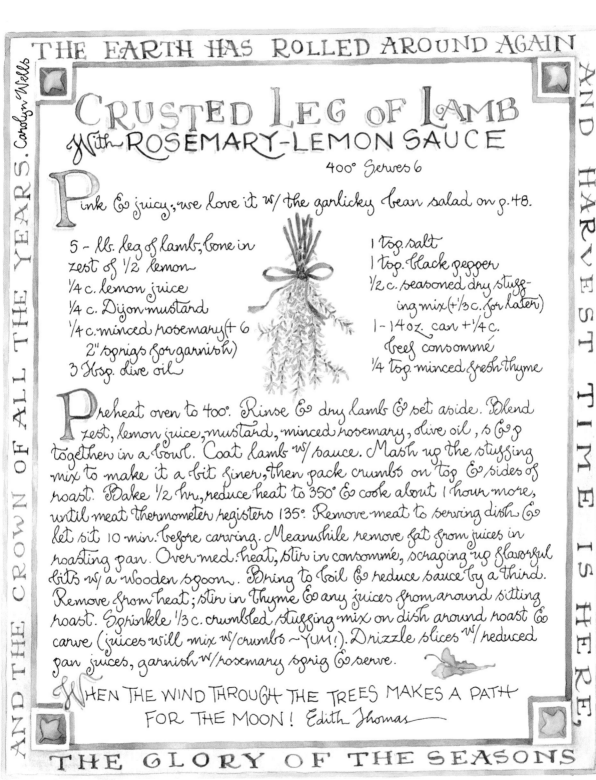

Carolyn Wells

CRUSTED LEG of LAMB
With ROSEMARY-LEMON SAUCE

400° Serves 6

Pink & juicy; we love it w/ the garlicky bean salad on p. 48.

5 - lb. leg of lamb, bone in
zest of ½ lemon
¼ c. lemon juice
¼ c. Dijon mustard
¼ c. minced rosemary (+ 6
    2" sprigs for garnish)
3 Tbsp. olive oil

1 tsp. salt
1 tsp. black pepper
½ c. seasoned dry stuff-
    ing mix (+⅓ c. for later)
1 - 14 oz. can + ¼ c.
    beef consommé
¼ tsp. minced fresh thyme

Preheat oven to 400°. Rinse & dry lamb & set aside. Blend zest, lemon juice, mustard, minced rosemary, olive oil, s & p together in a bowl. Coat lamb w/ sauce. Mash up the stuffing mix to make it a bit finer, then pack crumbs on top & sides of roast. Bake ½ hr., reduce heat to 350° & cook about 1 hour more, until meat thermometer registers 135°. Remove meat to serving dish & let sit 10 min. before carving. Meanwhile remove fat from juices in roasting pan. Over med. heat, stir in consommé, scraping up flavorful bits w/ a wooden spoon. Bring to boil & reduce sauce by a third. Remove from heat; stir in thyme & any juices from around sitting roast. Sprinkle ⅓ c. crumbled stuffing mix on dish around roast & carve (juices will mix w/ crumbs ~ YUM!). Drizzle slices w/ reduced pan juices, garnish w/ rosemary sprig & serve.

When the wind through the trees makes a path for the moon! Edith Thomas

Left margin: AND THE CROWN OF ALL THE YEARS.

Right margin: AND HARVEST TIME IS HERE,

PURE DINNER-PARTY FOOD, BUT PERFECT FOR
ANY ROMANTIC EVENING ♥

CLASSIC
Tenderloin of Beef
With Butter Croutons
SERVES 6

Easy, quick & delicious ~ sauce & croutons can be made ahead. Serve this w/ Roasted Fall Vegetables & Caramelized Onion Sauce (p. 43), or try it w/ Red Chili Onion Rings (p.29) & Wild Mushroom Ragout (p.53).

1 c. sour cream	3 Tbsp. canola oil
½ c. hot prepared horseradish	6 - 6 oz. beef tenderloin
1 long loaf sourdough bread	steaks (filet mignon)
3 Tbsp. butter	salt & pepper

Combine sour cream & horseradish; chill. Cut six ½" slices of bread. In a lg. skillet, over med. heat, melt butter w/oil. Fry bread, on one side only, 'til toasty brown. Remove from pan & drain, toasted side down, on p. towels. To same skillet, over med. high heat, add generously peppered steaks & cook on both sides 'til done the way you like them (if you cover the pan they'll cook faster). Sprinkle steaks w/salt. To serve, place a steak on top of a crouton & pass the horseradish sauce.)

TIP:
There is no known navy blue food. If there is navy blue food in the refrigerator, it signifies death. ♥ Erma Bombeck

84

WEATHERWISE, IT'S SUCH A GROOVY DAY. *Frank Sinatra* ♥

AUTUMN PICNIC MENU

LOBSTER ROLLS
POTATO SALAD
WARM BEAN SALAD
PORK RIBS
STUFFED EGGS
CORN BREAD
ICE CREAM
APPLE PIE
ARNOLD PALMERS

To make "Arnold Palmers": Mix together 2 parts iced tea w/ 1 part lemonade.

At last the day drifted into a long lacquered afternoon. *Edith Sitwell*

Morning Science

SPEAK TO THE EARTH
& IT SHALL TEACH THEE.
JOB XII.8

Every morning, for years & years & in all seasons, Joe & I walk the same walk ~ out a dirt road that meanders through the woods & around the pond, to road's end, where the pond opens to the sea ~ a place known locally as "the creek." Every season is wonderful there, but in the fall the woods dazzle us in reds & golds & woodsmoke spices the crisp ocean air. We bundle up, me in my green plaid scarf & Joe in his black beret.

After so many seasons, we feel intimate with every stick, tree & critter on the road. Over the years we have seen hawk, osprey, egret, owl, wild turkey, swan, deer, snake, Canada goose, bunny, lobster, skunk & of course, dog.

As we walk along we ask each other questions, trying to divine the secrets of nature. It's become a kind of game we call "Morning Science," which is FUNNY to us because we know NOTHING about science, something that has really come to light out there. That doesn't stop us ∵...

For example: MORNING SCIENCE, OCT. 12

ME: Look at the BIG hole in the trunk of that tree. Look how PERFECT it is ~ what do you s'pose made it?

JOE: A woodpecker?

ME: A WIDE-MOUTHED woodpecker?

JOE: How 'bout a beaver?

ME: Silence (I know there's no beavers here.)

(Now I see why people like to paint these adorable creatures...

I had to stop myself from putting little clothes on them. ♥)

JOE: How 'bout a man with a buzz saw?

END OF MORNING SCIENCE

Or

MORNING SCIENCE, SEPT. 17

ME: Look honey — look at the egret!
He's got part of his bill just SITTING in the
water. What do you think he's doing?

JOE: Eating.

ME: Possibly just imbibing? Don't they have to put their
heads under the water to SEE the food?

JOE (man of few words, especially in the morning): I don't
know.

END OF MORNING SCIENCE

And so it goes... we should probably call it "MORNING STUPID."
We may not know much about science, but we know
what we like. ♥ Critters do funny things in the
fall, things that don't happen any other time of year. One of the
hallmarks of the season is the giant flocks of starlings that show
up to hang out in the huge tree down the street from us. They do it
every year. They make so much noise I can hear them from inside
the house! I don't know how the people down there sleep! I know
they must wake up early, the bird clatter starts before sunrise.
When they aren't in that tree screaming at each other, they are swooping
& diving in unison through the neighborhood, up over the paint-spattered
maple trees & down to the low picket fences, just skimming the tops of
everything in a giant undulating black cloud of birds. It's beautiful,
but WHY DO THEY DO IT? I'll ask Joe... :

I hope you love birds, too.
It is economical. It saves
going to Heaven.
♥ Emily Dickinson

87

A LITTLE EDEN OF WOODS AND FIELDS...
MARK VAN DOREN

Sweater Weather
PLAY OUTSIDE

Keep an old sweater on a hook near the door ~ run outside to see the birds, the moon, lie under a tree as leaves fall.

Visit a corn maze or plan a hayride & end the day w/ a bonfire & roasted marshmallows.

The St. Francis of Assisi Blessing of the Animals celebrations take place around October 4th.

I LOVE YOU

Choose the PERFECT PUMPKIN at a farmstand or pumpkin farm ~ then have a taffy pull outdoors.

Leaf peep in your own neighborhood or plan a special trip to famously GORGEOUS New England & watch the leaves change color around old churches & graveyards.

There is no doubt that running away on a fresh blue morning can be exhilarating. ~ Jean Rhys

GO ON A WILD GOOSE CHASE...

Vermont

New England has a way of doing this to people; they can be homesick for it even if they have never seen it. ♥ MARK VAN DOREN

ANTIQUING IN NEW ENGLAND IS SO MUCH FUN! DISCOVER OLD BARNS & LITTLE STORES IN OLD HOUSES ON BACK ROADS...

WAITSFIELD

MOUNT WASHINGTON

Maine

MIDDLEBURY

LAKE WINNIPESAUKEE

WOODSTOCK

CAMDEN

CHRISTMAS COVE

PORTLAND

PORTSMOUTH

New Hampshire

ANDOVER

LEAF PEEPING

Joe & I pack the van, fill the ice chest with cucumber & roast beef sandwiches & off we go to wander the back roads of New England. We love the old graveyards, roadside stands, American flags, covered bridges & restaurants in old houses with slanted floors serving Indian Pudding bathed in cream in front of a fireplace. Here are a few of our favorite places. ♥

Massachusetts

LOUISA MAY ALCOTT HOUSE

CONCORD

SALEM

BOSTON

STOCKBRIDGE

NORMAN ROCKWELL MUSEUM

The Berkshires

STURBRIDGE ANTIQUES

RHODE ISLAND

PLYMOUTH FIRST THANKSGIVING 1621

MARK TWAIN HOUSE

LITCHFIELD HARTFORD

CAPE COD RT. 6A ANTIQUES

Connecticut

WICKFORD ANTIQUES

NEWPORT

NANTUCKET

ESSEX

← TO NYC

I do not own an inch of land, But all I see is mine. ♥ LUCY LARCOM

MARTHA'S VINEYARD

·89·

COUNTRY CLASSICS
FALL COLLECTIONS

One of a kind & hard to find ~ choose your poison & start a collection of your own! Fun to look for, especially when you find a "deal" ~ a charming way to make your home your own ♥.

Dish Towels

Wooden Cutting Boards

IN ANIMAL SHAPES

Striped Bowls

IRON BIRDS

SILHOUETTES

Bakelite

MIX & MATCH

in Autumn Colors

POTHOLDERS

Grab a friend, leaf peep while checking out yard sales, second-hand stores, flea markets & antique stores. Out with the "old," in with the "new" ~ do your part & have a yard sale yourself!

SWEETS

Something made of nothing,
tasting very sweet,
A most delicious compound,
with ingredients complete...
MARY E. BUELL

PEAR TATIN

375° Serves 8

Classic Autumn fare; pretty, old-fashioned, rustic & elegant, all in one~ DID I SAY "DELICIOUS"?

1-2 sheets frozen puff pastry ⋆
6 Tbsp. butter, softened
½ c. + 3 Tbsp. sugar

8 Bosc pears, peeled, halved & sliced lengthwise, ½" slices
Bourbon Praline (p.104) & vanilla ice cream~

Preheat oven to 375°. Thaw pastry (best used when still a bit frozen). Smear 4 Tbsp. butter & ½ c. sugar in bottom of a heavy 10" oven-proof skillet. Neatly arrange pears in circles, overlapping slices, starting at outside edge of skillet. Continue layering; then sprinkle on re-maining sugar & dot w/ butter. Cook pears over med. heat, shaking pan often to prevent sticking, until sugar mixture begins to turn golden (15-20 min.). Cut out a 10" round of pastry, press it gently over pears. Pierce w/ a knife. Place into oven 'til golden, about 20 min. With leaf-shaped cookie cutter, cut 3 leaves from remaining pastry, brush w/ milk & bake 10 min., till golden. (THIS IS A GOLDEN DESSERT!) When pastry is done place a slightly larger serving plate over skillet & quickly invert pie onto plate. Scatter pastry leaves over dessert. Serve hot w/ice cream & Bourbon Praline. (⋆ Roll out pastry if needed.)

A black cat dropped soundlessly from a high wall, like a spoonful of dark treacle, & melted under a gate.

ELIZABETH LEMARCHAND

IT'S ASTONISHING HOW SHORT A TIME IT TAKES FOR VERY WONDERFUL THINGS TO HAPPEN. ~ Frances Burnette

Gingerbread Cake

9 Servings

AROMATHERAPY: Tender, fragrant deliciousness, served warm in a puddle of LEMON SAUCE & topped w/ WHIPPED CREAM.

Lemon Sauce ~ MAKE THIS FIRST:

½ c. sugar
1 Tbsp. cornstarch
1 c. boiling water
3 Tbsp. fresh lemon juice
1 tsp. lemon zest
2 Tbsp. butter
dash of nutmeg

In a small saucepan, combine sugar & cornstarch. Gradually stir in boiling water. Cook & stir over med. heat 'til clear & thick. Blend in rest of ingred. Cover & refrigerate.

Whipped Cream

Just before serving, in a chilled bowl, using cold beaters, whip ½ pt. whipping cream w/ 1 Tbsp. sugar & 1 tsp. vanilla 'til soft peaks form.

Cake: PREHEAT 400°

1 c. sugar
2 Tbsp. molasses
1 tsp. cinnamon
1 tsp. salt
½ tsp. cloves
¼ tsp. ginger
4½ Tbsp. melted butter

1 egg
2 c. unbleached flour
1 tsp. baking soda
1 c. buttermilk

Preheat oven to 400°. Stir together first 7 ingred. Beat in egg. Sift flour & soda together & add alternately w/ buttermilk. Butter an 8" baking pan. Pour batter into pan & bake for 35 min. Cool slightly before serving (5 min.). Spoon Lemon Sauce onto dessert plates, set a square of warm cake in it & top w/ a dollop of whipped cream.

93

Cinnamon Ice Cream

MAKES 1½ QTS.

Easy & fun to make ~ keep a bowl of this in your freezer all season long ~ it goes with EVERYTHING: apple crisp to gingerbread cake. CAUTION: This recipe causes SPOON-IN-HAND disease.

1 c. brown sugar, firmly packed
2 Tbsp. butter
1 Tbsp. vanilla

1½ c. heavy cream
2 c. half & half
6 lg. egg yolks
1 tsp. cinnamon

BEST TO MEASURE EVERYTHING OUT FIRST

Put sugar, butter & vanilla in a saucepan over med. heat; stir 'til sugar melts & mixture is bubbly. Whisk in ½ c. heavy cream 'til smooth; remove from heat. In another pan combine 1 c. heavy cream w/ half & half & bring to simmer. Meanwhile, in a bowl, whisk egg yolks 'til blended. Whisk a small amount of warm cream mixture into yolks, warming them slowly while adding more cream ~ pour egg mixture back into pan w/ cream & stir constantly over low heat until mixture is slightly thickened, 3-4 min. (don't boil). Remove from heat immediately. Pour through fine mesh strainer into lg. bowl; whisk in brown sugar mixture & 1 tsp. cinnamon. Chill in fridge (or if you're in a hurry, put bowl into a larger bowl filled w/ ice & water); stir occasionally until cold. Freeze in ice cream maker.

Some of the days in November carry the whole memory of summer as a fire opal carries the color of moonrise. ✦ GLADYS TABER

Cranberry Apple Crisp

375° Serves 6

It doesn't get any better than this! ❤

4 lg. green apples,
  peeled & sliced 1/2"
1 c. fresh cranberries
3/4 c. brown sugar,
  firmly packed

1/2 c. flour
1/2 c. oats
3/4 tsp. cinnamon
3/4 tsp. nutmeg
1/3 c. softened butter

Preheat oven to 375°. Butter a square baking pan. Place apple slices & cranberries in the pan. Mix remaining ingred. well & sprinkle over fruit. Bake 30 min. Serve hot w/ice cream or cold with whipped cream. ❤

Indian Pudding

300° Serves 8

This old-fashioned pudding bakes for 3 hours, warming your kitchen & filling your house with the fragrance of cinnamon-spice & everything nice.

5½ c. whole milk
⅔ c. cornmeal
¼ c. butter
½ c. maple syrup
¼ c. molasses

1 tsp. ground ginger
1 tsp. cinnamon
½ tsp. salt
1 c. raisins
Vanilla ice cream

Preheat oven to 300°. Butter an 8"x8" baking dish. Over med. heat, in a large saucepan, heat the milk but don't boil it. Slowly whisk in cornmeal & continue to stir until mixture begins to thicken—about 10 min. Add next 7 ingred. & keep stirring 'til heated through. Pour into baking dish & bake 3 hrs. Serve warm w/ ice cream. (It's fine reheated.)

When I was a little girl, I always wanted to be in the kitchen, because it was warm, and that's where my mother was. ♡ Dolly Parton

OKTOBERFEST
Pumpkin Cheesecake

350° Serves 10-12

CRUST

3 c. broken gingersnaps
1 c. chopped pecans
1/4 c. sugar
2/3 c. melted butter

Preheat oven to 350°. In a food processor, finely grind cookies, nuts & sugar. Add butter; process until combined. Press mixture onto bottom & sides of 10" springform pan. Bake 10 min.

FILLING

4 - 8oz. pkgs. cream cheese, at room temp.
1 2/3 c. sugar
1 tsp. vanilla
1 15 oz. can pumpkin
2 Tbsp. whipping cream
2 Tbsp. rum

1 tsp. cinnamon
1/2 tsp. allspice
1/2 tsp. mace
1/2 tsp. ginger
1/2 tsp. cloves
4 lg. eggs
opt.: Bourbon Praline (p. 104)

Place a 9"x12" pan filled w/ water on lowest shelf in oven. With electric mixer beat together first 11 ingred. until smooth. Add eggs, one at a time, beating 'til just combined. Pour into crust, bake 1 hr. & 15 min., 'til puffy & light brown. Sprinkle w/ a little cinnamon, cool, then chill overnight. If desired, serve drizzled w/ a little Bourbon Praline.

LIVING NATURE, NOT DULL ART
SHALL PLAN MY WAYS & RULE MY HEART.
John Henry Cardinal Newman

Birthday Cake

350° Serves 12

A big, beautiful, elegant chocolate cake. Serve it to grown-ups with a glass of Bonny Doon Framboise. *mmmmmn*

16 oz. semisweet choc.	1 c. sugar
1 c. unsalted butter	unsweetened cocoa
1 Tbsp. orange zest	Chocolate Glaze (see below)
9 eggs	3/4 c. finely chopped walnuts

Preheat oven to 350°. Butter an 8½" springform pan; line the bottom w/ buttered wax paper, dust the pan w/cocoa. Over low heat in a heavy saucepan, slowly melt butter & chocolate; stir in zest & COOL. Meanwhile separate eggs into 2 LARGE bowls. Beat yolks about 1 minute, slowly add sugar  & continue beating until yolks are THICK & LEMON colored. Beat egg whites until they just begin to peak. Add COOLED choc. to egg yolks & blend thoroughly. Pour egg whites INTO choc. mixture & fold GENTLY until completely blended. Pour batter into prepared pan; bake 45 min. Cool ½ hr., turn out onto serving plate. Meanwhile make the

Chocolate Glaze

½ c. whipping cream	4 oz. semisweet choc., chopped
3 Tbsp. unsalted butter	4 oz. milk choc., chopped

Simmer cream & butter, reduce heat; add both chocolates & stir 'til smooth. Let stand 'til cool but still pourable, about 1 hr. Frost cake & cover entire top w/walnuts. Refrigerate 1 hr. to set glaze, but serve cake at room temp.

Fortune Cake

MAKING MAGIC

We felt so special & lucky when we found the dimes our mom used to bake into our BIRTHDAY cakes. ♥ Make your friends & family feel LUCKY too! I've always loved the idea of the old English custom of baking charms into holiday cakes, but I never knew where to get the CHARMS. I thought about stealing them from my Monopoly game ~ but then I found some inexpensive silver charms at a stationery store & now my collection looks like this. I just poke them down evenly throughout the batter. Get a collection of your own, but remember they have to bake in the oven ~ so don't use anything plastic!

AIRPLANE
YOU WILL TRAVEL

A REAL ACORN
LONG LIFE

A REAL WISHBONE
GOOD LUCK

LUCKY DIME PROSPERITY

PAPER CLIP
CAREER SUCCESS

A BELL
MENTAL CLARITY

RING
LOVE EVERLASTING

A REAL THIMBLE
A HAPPY HOME

There are only two ways to live your life. One is as though nothing is a miracle. The other is as if everything is.

ALBERT EINSTEIN

FRENCH ÉCLAIR WREATH

Serves 12 or more

A gorgeous way to feed a crowd ~ perfect for a buffet.

ZEE CRÈME

½ c. sugar
6 Tbsp. flour
¼ tsp. salt
2½ c. milk
2 egg yolks

1 Tbsp. butter
½ tsp. vanilla extract

ZEE CHANTILLY

½ c. whipping cream
1 Tbsp. sugar
1 tsp. vanilla extract

Mix sugar, flour & salt in top part of double boiler. Gradually stir in milk & cook over boiling water, stirring constantly 'til thickened. Cover & cook 10 min. longer, stirring occasionally. Beat egg yolks & add TO them a small amount of milk mixture. Warm the yolks in this way then return them to double boiler; cook 2 min. over hot, not boiling, water, stirring constantly. Remove from heat, stir in butter & ½ tsp. vanilla extract. Cool, film top w/plastic wrap & refrigerate. When cold, whip cream w/sugar & vanilla & fold into chilled crème.

ZEE WREATH

400°

1 c. water
3/4 c. butter

1 c. flour
4 eggs, room temp.

Preheat oven to 400°. Boil water & butter together. Remove from heat; add flour all at once, beating rapidly w/wooden spoon ↗

'til dough leaves side of Cool 5 min. Add eggs, frantically after each your arm falls off, whichever comes first. — pan & forms a ball. one at a time, beating until dough is smooth or Spoon dough onto an ungreased baking sheet in the shape of a 10" ring, leave it high & don't smooth top. Bake 40 min., turn off oven, keep door closed for another 15 min. Remove from oven, cool. Cut horizontally around ring & remove top. Gently pull out any wet filaments inside (only the bigger, easy-to-remove ones).

Glaze au Chocolat

7½ oz. good semisweet chocolate
5 tbsp. butter

Melt together in a heavy pan. Cool to thicken a bit, but pour over wreath while still warm. (See below.)

Fini

3 sliced bananas
¼ c. sliced almonds

Fill bottom of wreath w/ sliced bananas & cover with crème. Put the top back on wreath, drizzle chocolate over, sprinkle on the almonds. Refrigerate 'til serving time.

Voilà!

I GENERALLY AVOID TEMPTATION UNLESS I CAN'T RESIST IT.
♥ Mae West

Toasted Snowballs
in Chocolate Sauce

You can use store-bought everything & make this a very quick, elegant & easy make-ahead dessert, **or** you can go crazy & make the delicious Cinnamon Ice Cream on p. 94 & the outrageous Chocolate Sauce on p. 103. Either way: yum yum.

Preheat oven to 350°. Spread sweetened coconut on a cookie sheet & bake 5-10 min. Watch closely, stir occasionally 'til toasted. Roll ice cream balls in coconut & keep them in freezer. Serve a snowball in a puddle of chocolate sauce.

THE AIR IS AS COOL AS AN OLD COIN TEASPOON & A FAINT TANG OF BLUE WOODSMOKE SPICES THE WIND.

Gladys Taber

'TIS AN ILL COOK THAT CANNOT LICK HIS OWN FINGERS. WM. SHAKESPEARE

Chocolate Sauce
MAKES 1½ CUPS

3/4 c. milk
1 Tbsp. butter
3 oz. unsweetened chocolate

1½ c. sugar
3 Tbsp. light corn syrup
1 tsp. vanilla

Heat milk over low heat & melt butter & choc. in it, stirring constantly 'til smooth. Add in sugar & corn syrup & cook, stirring for 5 min. Stir in vanilla. Serve hot or cold. Keep in fridge.

Royal Icing

This pure white icing hardens as it dries ~ mix it w/ food coloring to decorate holiday cookies. It's also the "glue" that holds gingerbread houses together. Combine 1 lg. egg white w/ 1½ c. powdered sugar. Beat on high speed 10-15 min. 'til soft peaks form. Makes 3/4 c. Cover w/ plastic wrap when not in use. (If you are concerned about raw eggs, look for powdered egg whites at your gourmet food store.)

Bourbon Praline

Makes 2 c.

Drizzle this versatile, perfect-for-the-season sauce over baked apple, ice cream, or bread pudding—good hot or cold.

½ c. pecans, toasted & chopped
2 Tbsp. butter
¼ c. sugar
¼ c. + 1 Tbsp. brown sugar

2 Tbsp. molasses
2 Tbsp. dark corn syrup
⅓ c. heavy cream
2 tsp. bourbon

Toast pecans in a dry skillet over med. heat, shaking & stirring often. Chop & set aside. Put next 5 ingred. into a small saucepan over low heat; stir until sugar is dissolved (about 5 min.); do not boil. Stir in other ingred., including pecans. Serve hot or cold.

Ginger Crisp Ice Cream Sandwiches

Make Ginger Crisps on p. 106. Use a glass or a cookie cutter to make 4" rounds. When cool, place a 1" slab of Cinnamon Ice Cream (p. 94) between 2 cookies. Smooth sides. Wrap in wax paper & keep frozen.

Bananas & Tipsy Cream

To make BOURBON ICE CREAM, make Cinnamon Ice Cream p. 94 but delete cinnamon & add in ¼ c. + 1 Tbsp. bourbon. Put 1 ripe banana per person on a cookie sheet & into a 350° oven for 20 min. 'til skin turns black. Slit skin open & moosh up (as you would w/a baked potato). Serve hot w/ice cream & a sprinkle of fresh ground coffee. YUM!

104

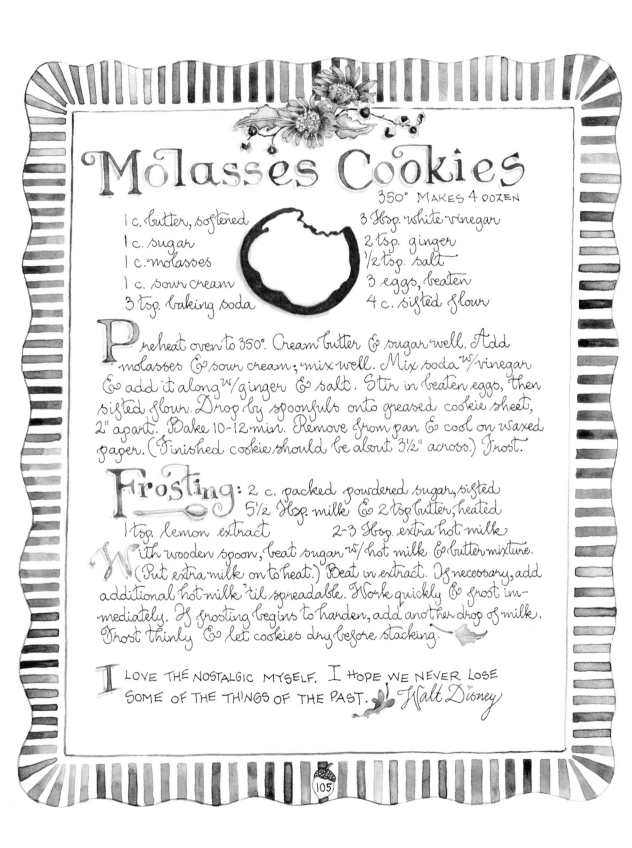

Molasses Cookies

350° MAKES 4 DOZEN

1 c. butter, softened
1 c. sugar
1 c. molasses
1 c. sour cream
3 tsp. baking soda

3 Tbsp. white vinegar
2 tsp. ginger
½ tsp. salt
3 eggs, beaten
4 c. sifted flour

Preheat oven to 350°. Cream butter & sugar well. Add molasses & sour cream; mix well. Mix soda w/vinegar & add it along w/ginger & salt. Stir in beaten eggs, then sifted flour. Drop by spoonfuls onto greased cookie sheet, 2" apart. Bake 10-12 min. Remove from pan & cool on waxed paper. (Finished cookie should be about 3½" across.) Frost.

Frosting:
2 c. packed powdered sugar, sifted
5½ Tbsp. milk & 2 tsp. butter, heated
1 tsp. lemon extract   2-3 Tbsp. extra hot milk

With wooden spoon, beat sugar w/ hot milk & butter mixture. (Put extra milk on to heat.) Beat in extract. If necessary, add additional hot milk 'til spreadable. Work quickly & frost immediately. If frosting begins to harden, add another drop of milk. Frost thinly & let cookies dry before stacking.

I LOVE THE NOSTALGIC MYSELF. I HOPE WE NEVER LOSE SOME OF THE THINGS OF THE PAST. *Walt Disney*

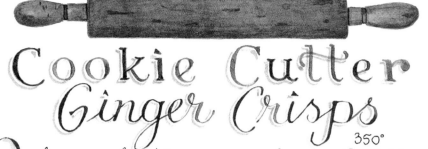

Cookie Cutter
Ginger Crisps

350°

I always make these spicy cookies in September ~ I freeze them & use them all season; here's why: You can cut them into acorn, pear & leaf shapes & serve them with tea or cocoa; or decorate a dessert plate. They make darling placecards when you write your guests' names on them in Royal Icing (p. 103). Roll them a little thinner & they make a beautiful sweet cracker; serve them w/a dessert cheese such as St. Andre as an appetizer. Cut into tiny hearts or stars & float them on top of ice cream, pudding, pumpkin pie, or even in salads. Or make Ginger Crisp Ice Cream Sandwiches (p. 104). Make bats, witches, cats, gingerbread men & numbers for a birthday cake.

1 c. softened butter	4½ c. sifted flour
½ c. brown sugar, firmly packed	1½ tsp. cinnamon
	1½ tsp. ginger
½ c. sugar	1 tsp. salt
⅓ c. molasses	1 tsp. baking soda
⅔ c. light corn syrup	½ tsp. ground cloves

Preheat oven to 350°. Cream butter & sugars until light. Add molasses & corn syrup & stir well. Add in the rest of ingred. & knead until smooth. Chill well. Roll out on a lightly floured surface to less than 1/8" thick. Cut w/floured cutters. Bake on greased cookie sheet for 8 min. Cool & store in airtight container, or freeze them (they thaw in just moments).

And when all of the flourless chocolate cakes & chocolate mousse or ganache cakes have come & gone, there will still be nothing like a fudgy brownie, dry & crackled on top, moist & dense within, with a glass of cold milk. ~ RICHARD SAX

BROWNIES

THE BEST!   325° Makes 12

2 oz. (squares) unsweetened chocolate   pinch of salt
1/3 c. butter (5½ Tbsp.)   ½ c. flour
3/4 c. sugar   3/4 c. walnuts, chopped
1 egg   1 tsp. vanilla

Preheat oven to 325°. Butter an 8" square pan well. Melt chocolate & butter in lg. saucepan. Stir in rest of ingred. in order given. Spread in pan. Bake 30 min. Cool completely for chewiest results (this will require WILL POWER!) ~ pour the milk.

I LOVED GOING BACK TO SCHOOL IN THE FALL. EVERY-THING ABOUT IT SMELLED GOOD TO ME ~ MY NEW NOTEBOOK FILLED WITH DELICIOUS-SMELLING LINED PAPER, NEW CLOTHES & SHOES, MY HAIR FRESHLY BRAIDED ~ I LOVED THE SMELL OF THE "CLOAK ROOM" WHERE ALL THE SACK LUNCHES WERE KEPT, WARM BALONEY SANDWICHES & BROWNIES, CUT-UP ORANGES & THERMOS BOTTLES FULL OF CHOCOLATE MILK, FROM MOMS WHO LOVED US.

AFTERNOON TEA

MY KITCHEN LINOLEUM IS SO BLACK & SHINY THAT I WALTZ WHILE I WAIT FOR THE KETTLE TO BOIL. ♥ *Florida Scott-Maxwell*

TIME OUT

LET THE DANCE BEGIN

When the clock strikes four, fill a kettle with fresh water & bring it to a boil. Fill a tea ball with good tea such as Earl Grey. Let it steep in your teapot 3~5 min. Make "tea" simple or more elaborate — here are a few good things to have on hand:

CUTE CUPS

DUCK

HALF & HALF

LEMON SLICES

SUGAR

HONEY

SHE HAD A CURIOUS SENSE

OF HER OWN ROOTS TWINED ABOUT THE OLD HOUSE.
AFTER ALICE TISDALE HOBART

YUMMY CREAM SCONES (p.109)

LEMON CURD

CLOTTED CREAM

CINNAMON TOAST

ORANGE MARMALADE

KEEP THE POT WARM WITH A TEA COZY.

Good alone, with a best friend, & fun for a party — we celebrated our 9th anniversary with an "Anniversary Tea."

FINGER SANDWICHES
CUCUMBER, EGG & RADISH

"It was the usual "Zoo tea." You know, we eat, the others watch."
— PRINCESS MARGARET

See Tea (w/ a capital "T") done the "right way" in London at Brown's, The Savoy, Grosvenor House, or upstairs at Harrods. Bring back memories & make

HEART-SHAPED
Cream Scones
425° MAKES 10

2 c. flour
1/3 c. sugar
1 Tbsp. baking powder

1 tsp. salt
1/2 c. currants (opt.)
1 c. heavy cream

Preheat oven to 425°. Stir together first 5 ingred. Gradually stir in cream. Gather dough together & knead lightly on a floured board; this will start off seeming impossible, but don't give up. Pat out to 1/2" thick. Cut w/ a 2" heart-shaped cutter dipped in flour. Arrange on ungreased baking sheet. Bake 10-12 min. 'til golden. You can GLAZE them w/ a creamy mixture of 1/2 c. powdered sugar, 1 tsp. orange zest & about 1 Tbsp. fresh o.j. Serve hot with

Orange Butter: With a wooden spoon beat together 1 stick unsalted butter (softened), 2 Tbsp. frozen o.j. concentrate, zest of 1/2 orange, 1/4 c. + 1 Tbsp. powdered sugar. Spoon into ramekin & smooth top.

She has got on to the right side of the baking powder, and her cakes and things are so light they fly down your throat of themselves.
— Susan Hale

AN AUTUMN DO-BEE

CINNAMON SUGAR
3 TBSP. SUGAR
1/2 tsp. CINNAMON
PUT ALL IN SHAKER
JAR + KEEP NEAR
TOASTER

109

HOMEMADE Marshmallows

MAKES 64 1" SQUARE MARSHMALLOWS
YOU WILL NEED A CANDY THERMOMETER

Roast 'em at a hayride bonfire or melt them in hot chocolate (p.111). Mmmm-mmmm-good!

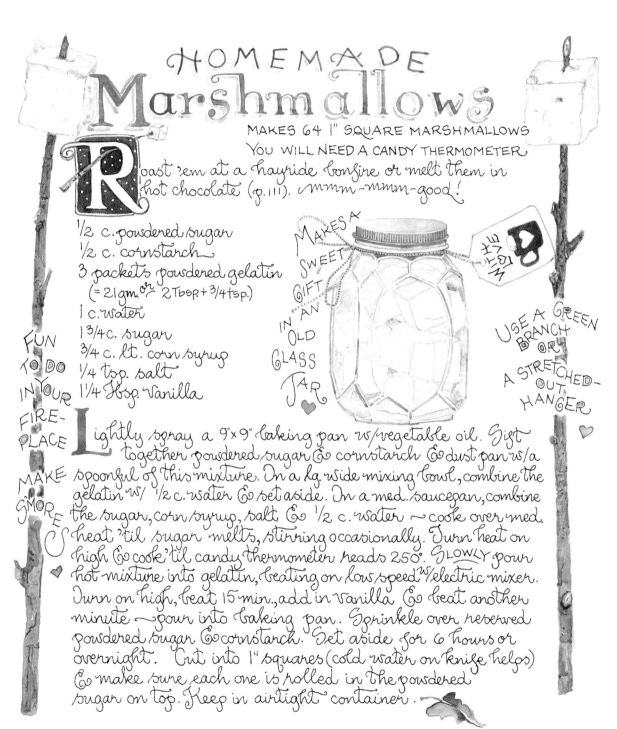

½ c. powdered sugar
½ c. cornstarch
3 packets powdered gelatin
  (= 21 gm. or 2 Tbsp. + ¾ tsp.)
1 c. water
1¾ c. sugar
¾ c. lt. corn syrup
¼ tsp. salt
1¼ Tbsp. vanilla

MAKES A SWEET GIFT IN AN OLD GLASS JAR

WITH LOVE

USE A GREEN BRANCH OR A STRETCHED-OUT HANGER

FUN TO DO IN YOUR FIRE-PLACE

MAKE S'MORES

Lightly spray a 9"×9" baking pan w/ vegetable oil. Sift together powdered sugar & cornstarch & dust pan w/ a spoonful of this mixture. In a lg. wide mixing bowl, combine the gelatin w/ ½ c. water & set aside. In a med. saucepan, combine the sugar, corn syrup, salt & ½ c. water ~ cook over med. heat 'til sugar melts, stirring occasionally. Turn heat on high & cook 'til candy thermometer reads 250°. SLOWLY pour hot mixture into gelatin, beating on low speed w/ electric mixer. Turn on high, beat 15 min., add in vanilla & beat another minute ~ pour into baking pan. Sprinkle over reserved powdered sugar & cornstarch. Set aside for 6 hours or overnight. Cut into 1" squares (cold water on knife helps) & make sure each one is rolled in the powdered sugar on top. Keep in airtight container.

Hot Chocolate

Always use the best quality chocolate you can find. This is the kind of hot chocolate you DREAM about.

PER 8 OZ. CUP:

1 oz. unsweetened chocolate   1 c. hot milk
1 tbsp. sugar   freshly whipped cream

Finely grate or shave the chocolate or put it in the food processor (steel blade). Put the chocolate in a mug, add sugar & whisk in hot milk. This chocolate should be served w/ a huge dollop of whipped cream & a spoon. A peppermint stick makes a good stirrer.

Cocoa Mix

This is the chocolate you serve w/ the Homemade Marshmallows on p. 110. Pack this into jars & tie on homemade tags for hostess gifts.

MIXTURE:

3/4 c. unsweetened cocoa
3/4 c. sugar
1/2 tsp. cinnamon
1/2 c. crushed peppermint candy (opt.)

Mix all ingred. & keep in airtight container.

TO MAKE COCOA:

Add 2 tbsp. Cocoa Mix to 8 oz. (1 c.) hot milk; stir until dissolved. Pour hot cocoa over 2 fresh marshmallows. Good with cinnamon toast.

FOR:
CHILLY NIGHTS
WARM FIRE
FULL MOON
OLD SONGS
EASY CHAIR
SOFT WORDS
SWEET DREAMS

Autumn Spiced Cider

½ gal. apple cider
2 c. orange juice
3 - 3" cinnamon sticks
10 whole cloves
zest of 1 orange
¼ tsp. ground nutmeg
¼ tsp. ground allspice

She (the cat) hasn't had her full ration of kisses-on-the-lips today. ...she had the half-past-six one in the garden, but she's missed tonight's.
— Colette

Bring all ingred. to a boil, boil 15 min. Strain through fine mesh into thermos or back into pan. Serve hot.

COLD and FLU SEASON

Put a shot of Jack Daniel's in a big mug—add a teaspoon of honey, the juice of one lemon & fill it with boiling water. Rub Vicks on your chest, tie a sock around your neck, put cotton in your ears, get your kitty & go to bed with the clicker. When you feel well enough to eat, have Campbell's Chicken Noodle Soup, buttered saltines & 7-Up. FEEL BETTER SOON!

We cough because we can't help it, BUT OTHERS DO IT ON PURPOSE. ♥ Mignon McLaughlin

EVERY LITTLE WAVE HAS ITS NIGHTCAP ON.
Laura Howe Richards

Hot Toddies

after ~ *dinner*

and

COFFEES

PUMPKIN LATTE

2 heaping Tbsp. canned pumpkin
1 Tbsp. brown sugar
1 tsp. vanilla extract
½ tsp. pumpkin pie spice
hot coffee, decaf, or espresso
hot milk

Into each lg. mug put first 4 ingred. Fill cup halfway w/coffee & stir well. Fill cup w/ hot milk & whisk. Top w/ whipped cream, dust w/nutmeg.

EGGNOG CAPPUCCINO

Steam eggnog (instead of milk). Spoon onto cappuccino & dust w/cinnamon.

A KISS-IN-THE-DARK

Into each mug put 1 oz. of brandy & 1 oz. of kahlua. Fill w/ hot coffee & top w/ lots of whipped cream.

· A TOAST ·

DAWN LOVE IS SILVER, WAIT FOR THE WEST:
OLD LOVE IS GOLD LOVE ~ OLD LOVE IS BEST.
Katherine Lee Bates

113

COCKTAILS

My BROTHERS & SISTERS & I AREN'T AS CONCERNED WITH EACH OTHER'S COOTIES AS WE WERE WHEN WE WERE KIDS, BUT EVERYONE DOES GET THEIR OWN STRAW!

HARVEST MOON
MAKES 2 DRINKS

½ c. sweet & sour
½ c. carbonated water
¼ c. apricot brandy
4 tsp. pomegranate juice

Put 1st 3 ingred. in a cocktail shaker w/ ice. Shake well & strain into martini glasses. Gently pour 2 tsp. pomegranate juice into each glass—do not stir. (Also good served over ice.)

Hand in hand, on the edge of the sand They danced by the light of the moon...
— EDWARD LEAR

VAMPIRE'S KISS

½ c. Redrum (spiced rum)
1 c. cranberry juice cocktail
¼ c. triple sec
2 red maraschino cherries

Shake 1st 3 ingred. w/ crushed ice. Strain into 2 martini glasses & pop in the cherries (KISS).

'Twas a Dark and Stormy Night

On Martha's Vineyard, Mother Nature gives us perfect Halloween weather ~ a cold windy night with leaves flying in a black starlit sky. Deep shadows from tall hedges, & rustling leaves in every corner make it eerie & very scary. Halloween candles light the old houses & glowing pumpkins leer or cheer on every porch. Windblown Batmen, dalmatians & bumblebees hold tight to bags of candy as they run from house to house, steering clear of the darkest shadows where everyone knows the goblins are waiting to GITcha! Muffled voices call to one another in a wild street scene; flashlight beams bounce off walkways & curbs (AND HIM! →) while mommies & daddies stand nearby as islands of safety for big-eyed babies in bunny suits.

The kids have a wonderful time but we know their parents need sustenance too ~ so we make a big pot of steaming Spiced Cider (p. 112) & offer it in hand-warming hot-cups-to-go, with or without a little bit of spiced rum (the rum turns it into an "UNDERTAKER").

I WENT OUT TO TAKE PICTURES AND SAW THIS COMING UP THE STREET. IT NEVER SAID A WORD, JUST KEPT COMING. I SNAPPED THIS PHOTO AND RAN AWAY! BRYYYY...

It's all over by 10 o'clock & we're feet-up in front of the fireplace, with our own cups of cider, listening to the wind while embers pop softly & the Halloween candles burn down. All the creatures of the night are safe in bed (we hope!) & we're next.

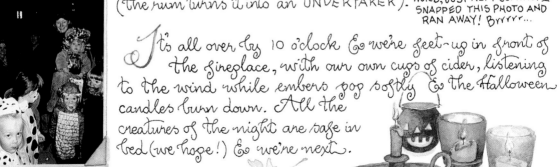

OUR FRONT DOOR

KNOCK-KNOCK. WHO'S THERE? BOO! BOO WHO? OH, DON'T CRY!

Be Afraid, Be Very Afraid

In our family of 8 children, Halloween was a very big deal, even though we did the scary-story thing year-round. Camping or sleeping out in the backyard required ghost stories & my dad was (and is) a master of storytelling. He scared what he called "the bejeebers" out of us with his stories about trolls that lived under the bridge, the mind-blowing, child-eating Hobias & the homicidal maniac that comes up the stairs, starting in the basement, ONE-STEP-AT-A-TIME, until he's GOT YOU!

But my favorite fright night took place at a Girl Scout Halloween party when I was about 11. We were seated in a half-circle out in the garage with a leader at each end & the storyteller facing us in the middle. There were towels placed in our laps & all the lights were turned off. Mrs. Johnson (obviously a sick person, just like my dad) began to tell us about a dark & stormy night when a man named John Brown, who lived just up the street, was murdered by an escaped convict. She did this in a slow, low voice. "They never found Mr. Brown's body" (she told us in that pitch-dark garage), "only pieces of it buried all over town. We're going to identify the body tonight & bring it back together so the ghost of Mr. Brown can stop wandering the neighborhood late at night knocking on doors." (Right then she KNOCK-KNOCKED on a piece of wood!) "Brrrr," she said, & then she told us, "Here are the remains of John Brown" & began passing his body parts down the line. "First they found one of his ears" (& in the dark we felt a dried apricot); "& then, his nose" (a cold raw chicken wing); "now here are his brains" (a bowl with wet squishy tomatoes). "They found both eyeballs" (two large, cold, peeled grapes) — THIS IS THE ONE THAT ALMOST DID ME IN, BUT IT GOT WORSE WHEN SHE SAID, "and here's

his liver," which was a hunk of raw liver (no bowl) passed down the line. OH MY GOD. "They found his hair too" (a piece of wet fur) & "here's his hand" (a latex glove filled w/ice-cold mud) & last but not least, "here are the WORMS that ate the rest of him" (a bowl of overcooked spaghetti, cut up & dressed with a little veg. oil). Then she said, "That's all we found... now, repeat after me: On Halloween night •
the banshee howls •
now poor John Brown •
is wrapped in towels •
GOODNIGHT, JOHN!"

We jumped out of our socks when they suddenly struck matches to relight the pumpkins, but soon we were laughing again & off we went to bob for apples, throats parched from all the SCREAMING!

I DON'T EVEN WANT TO TELL YOU WHICH ONE IS ME! (TALK ABOUT SCARY!)

That's the real trouble with the world, too many people grow up. They forget. They don't remember what it's like to be twelve years old.
— Walt Disney

HALLOWEEN 1939
UNCLE DICK, MY MOM, UNCLE BOB

WITCHES BREW

Children's Halloween Punch

Makes 12 - 8oz. cups

Light, not-too-sweet apple cranberry sparkler, but the coup de grace is the FLOATING HAND! Brrrr! Big people like this too.

2 frozen hands (see below)
4 c. white cranberry juice
3 c. apple juice

½ c. lime juice
3½ c. carbonated water
1 c. pineapple tidbits
opt. garnish: thin slices of lime

Make hands first & put in the freezer. Mix all remaining ingred. & chill well. Pour into lg. punch bowl & at last moment, float frozen hand in punch.

Floating Hands

Rinse out 1 pair of vinyl gloves very well. Remove stems from 10 maraschino cherries & rinse them. Put a little water into the gloves & work a cherry into each fingertip ~ fill gloves w/ water (not too full). Tie ends of gloves tightly into knots; put them flat on plates & freeze completely. Cut off knots, peel off gloves & float in punch. (Save 2nd one for when 1st one melts ♥.)

WHEN WE WOULD RIDE, WE TAKE WINDLE-STRAWS, OR BEANSTALKS, AND PUT THEM BETWIXT OUR FEET, AND SAY THRICE: HORSE AND HATTOCK, HORSE AND GO, HORSE AND PELLATTIS, HO! HO! AND IMMEDIATELY WE WOULD FLY AWAY WHEREVER WE WOULD.
Isobel Cowdie (1662)

TRICK OR TREAT
DINNER MENU
CORN PUDDING (p.54)
RAINBOW JELL-O (p.67)
MOLASSES COOKIES (p.105)
HALLOWEEN PUNCH

Eat, Drink and Be Scary

IDEAS FOR HALLOWEEN FUN

HALLOWEEN DINNER MENU
* TOUCHDOWN CHILI (p.78)
* IOWA CORN BREAD (p.61)
* CURRIED PUMPKIN POTS (p.51)
* GINGERBREAD CAKE WITH LEMON SAUCE (p.93)
* CINNAMON ICE CREAM (p.94)

* Use a hollowed-out pumpkin as an ice bucket.
* Freeze plastic spiders in ice cubes.
* Hide toy eyeballs in the spiced-nut bowl.
* Use actual tree twigs (strong ones) for caramel apples.

* Make your chili scarier: put sour cream in sandwich bag, squeeze down, & snip off corner. Make three concentric circles on top of each bowl of chili ~ draw a knife through sour cream to make a spider web.

* Make kitchen magic for your little ones: prepare milk glasses by putting a drop of food coloring in each ~ say "ABRACADABRA" as you pour milk into glasses. USE YOUR MAGIC WAND.

* RED is a great color for an elegant Halloween party ~ start w/ a Vampire's Kiss (p. 114); have red roses, red candles, red wine, red light bulbs, BURN edges of placecards & invitations, tie napkins w/ black ribbons, have guests wear red or black.

* Use hollowed-out horned melons for dips.

* Eat candy corn or popcorn out of a giant hurricane lamp while watching Halloween classics such as Beetlejuice, The Canterbury Ghost, Bell, Book & Candle, or my favorite, Practical Magic.

WIND GIVES SPEECH TO TREES.
HELEN AOKI KANEKO

Tree Talk

Advice from a tree:

STAND TALL. ACT NATURALLY. ENJOY THE VIEW. SETTLE DOWN. MAKE YOURSELF USEFUL. CHANGE YOUR LOOK FOR THE SEASON. SMELL GOOD. SINK DEEP ROOTS. YOU NEVER LOOK STUPID BY STAYING QUIET. LEARN TO BEND. TAKE WHAT COMES AND MAKE THE BEST OF IT. DRINK PLENTY OF WATER. RECYCLE. BE YOURSELF. TAKE THE WINTER OFF.

I'll give you the whole megillah in a one-word speech:

Reach.
—Frank Sinatra

THE FOREST'S AFIRE! THE FOREST'S AFIRE! THE MAPLE IS BURNING, TH
CAMORE'S TURNING, THE BEECH IS ALIGHT. *Eleanor Farjeon* ELM · LAR
WEET GUM · POPLAR · MULBERRY · APPLE · DOGWOOD · BIRCH · BAY LAUREL · PLUM
NDEN · WEEPING CHERRY · ASH · HAWTHORN · APRICOT · SUGAR MAPLE · PEA
GLISH WALNUT · HOLLY OAK · PERSIMMON · SWEET BUCKEYE · MAGNOLIA · OLIV
BIZZIA · HICKORY · JAPANESE ELM · QUINCE · LARCH · CRABAPPLE · MIMOSA
G · PECAN · CHINESE PRIVET · DOGWOOD · BAY LAUREL · LINDEN · EUCALYPTUS · A
QUIDAMBAR · SYCAMORE · WEEPING WILLOW · OAK · ACACIA · ELM · ALBIZZI
H · MULBERRY · CRABAPPLE · APRIC   WEET GUM · OLIVE · ASPEN · SUMACH · YE
TTERNUT · BEECH · SUGAR MAP   OLIA · SWEET BUCKEYE · MAGNOLIA
AR · BAY LAUREL · QUI   RAE · ENGLISH WALNUT · OA

LET THERE BE LIGHT

PEN · PERSIMMON · ASH   IMOSA · DOGWOOD · QUINC
ANESE ELM · JUNIPER   DAMBAR · OAK · HAWTHORN

As October ends, most of the branches are bare. We see more sky.
Gladys Taber

LMOND · PLUM · HORSE C   FIG · BEECH · POPLAR · ASPE
MACH · YEW · LINDEN · A   OLIVE · BAY LAUREL · APPLE
M · SWEET GUM · MAPL   IMMON · WEEPING CHERR
ARCH · DOGWOOD · PECA   ACACIA · GUM · BUTTERNU
UINCE · SWEET BUCKE   · MAGNOLIA · FIG · LINDE
WTHORN · ALBIZZIA · MULBERRY · PEAR · SUGAR MAPLE · CHERRY
E SWAMP MAPLES TURN FIRST AND THEIR COLOR IS INCREDIBLE. T
REALLY BURN WITH COLOR. *Gladys Taber* SCARLET, PALE GOLD AND
NNAMON · SYCAMORE · RED BUD MAPLE · SWEET GUM · QUINCE · O
EECH · HORSE CHESTNUT · BAY LAUREL · LIQUIDAMBAR · WHITE BIRC
UM · HICKORY · ASH · GUM · BUTTERNUT · CRABAPPLE · HOLLY OAK · EL
LACK WALNUT · PECAN · LINDEN · SUMACH · OAK · MULBERRY · ASPE
RICOT · BEECH · LEAVES ARE VERBS THAT CONJUGATE THE SEASONS.
tyl Ehrlich · SUGAR MAPLE · PERSIMMON · CHINESE PRIVET · BUTTER
CAMORE · LARCH · ELM · APPLE · FIG · OLIVE · ENGLISH WALNUT · HICKOR
AGNOLIA · ALBIZZIA · POPLAR · WEEPING CHERRY · MAGNOLIA · A

WE HAVE A LITTLE FARM IN CALIFORNIA WHERE WE HOPE TO RETIRE SOMEDAY.
OUR DREAM IS TO START A LITTLE COOKING SCHOOL THERE. WE COULD PUT IT
IN THE BARN. JOE COULD TEACH THE REAL COOKING, & I COULD TEACH 12-YEAR-
OLDS HOMEMAKING. I WOULD LOVE THAT. ♥

If there were dreams to sell,
Merry and sad to tell,
And the crier rung his bell,
What would you buy?

T.L. BEDDOES

Although Autumn doesn't officially
end for another 2 weeks, somebody
forgot to tell Old Man Winter to check his
calendar ~ we woke up this morning to several
inches of snow, it's still snowing, big fat flakes
floating down like polka dots, a winter wonderland. First thing
we did is scramble into our layers; hats, scarves, gloves, &
out we went on our daily woods-walk-to-the-sea ~ intrepid New
Englanders ~ neither sleet nor snow nor whatever-it-is, will keep us
from our appointed rounds ~ or from playing in the first snow of
the season! (Joe took my picture to show you) We're home now, Joe made
us a fire; he's gone back out to shovel a path to the barn.

This snow has me thinking about Christmas. We're going out to
California in a couple of weeks ~ after I turn in the pages for this
book. When we travel to California, we go by train. At this time of year
it can be quite an adventure ~ the train station all huffing & puffing
with smoke & steam from the trains, everyone bundled up, all the
excitement of the coming & going. The train slowly pulls out

THE FIRST TIME I WENT ON A TRIP WITH JOE, I ASKED
HIM, "WHAT SHALL I BRING?" HE SAID, "EVERYTHING." ♥

TA-DAAA

of the station, swaying through the snow ~ we're all cozy inside for the 3-day trip, which I have always loved despite uncertainty due to the nature of the train system. (I keep wishing that Disney would buy Amtrak!) I feel so peaceful on the train; I love the books I get to bring along, love the view from our little room, farm fields covered in snow, cornstalks still standing in rows, sunrises & sunsets from our window. We've seen every season from those windows. But a couple of years ago, we discovered the most amazing thing ~ at Christmastime this entire country is covered in holiday lights from sea to shining sea. From our train-room-with-a-view, we ooohed & aaahed all the way 'cross country, watching the "light show" go by. From big sparkling cities w/ skyscrapers & trees covered head to toe in white lights, to tiny houses out in the middle of nowhere w/ just one little string of colored lights on the porch ~ it felt like the whole world was connected.

We stopped in Chicago for a few hours; Joe went out & got us a string of lights for our room, so we could return the favor to everyone who lives near the tracks.

I hear Joe now, he's out on the porch making crunching noises with his boots, so I'm going to throw another log on the fire, go make us some tea & say farewell to Autumn (& to you), (FOR NOW!), say HELLO to Winter, a little early, the season especially suited to DREAMING.

I suppose you can't have everything, though my instinctive response to this sentiment is always, "Why not?" Margaret Halsey

ONE WORLD

123

Thank You

FOR YOUR EXPERTISE WITH LOVE TO MARY HICKEY · JEFF MARCOVE JEREMY LIMPIC KELLEE RASOR PAM PETERSEN HELEN ROSSIER MARCELLE BEN·DAVID & R.R. DONNELLY ♥ ♥

TO MY DEAREST FRIENDS · ELAINE SULLIVAN · LORRIE DOMINGUEZ · CLIFF BRANCH · MARGOT DATZ · DIANA BOWLBY · ELIZABETH NORDLINGER · SHARON LOVEJOY · JEFF PROSTOVICH · LOWLY GARCIA · JANET & TIM HALEY · JANE BAY · MARTHA YUKOVICH · ANNIE FOLEY · SUSAN RIOS · JAIME HAMLIN · AURELIA KOBY · RACHEL ASHBY · JOHN ANDERSON · MARJORIE LAU · JEI THAYER ·

FOR YOUR BEAUTIFUL LETTERS, YOUR STORIES, YOUR SUPPORT, LOVE AND INSPIRATION, MY READERS "THE GIRLFRIENDS" AS I CALL YOU — WHICH INCLUDES THE GUYS — THANK YOU FROM THE BOTTOM OF MY HEART.

One only leaf upon the top of a tree — the sole remaining leaf — danced round & round like a rag blown by the wind. *Dorothy Wordsworth*

TO ALL THE FOLKS AT LITTLE, BROWN. I CAN'T BELIEVE IT'S BEEN 19 YEARS! MUCH APPRECIATION & GRATITUDE TO EVERYONE BUT ESPECIALLY MARY TONDORF-DICK, MY EDITOR FOR ALL THESE YEARS; TO JENNIFER BRENNAN · MICHAEL PIETSCH · HEATHER RIZZO & JEAN GRIFFIN · MARILYN DOOF · PEG ANDERSON · SOPHIE COTTRELL ·

FOR ALL THE FUN ♥ TO MY FAMILY: MOM AND DAD, JIM, STEVE, CHUCK, BRAD, PAUL A., MARY AND SHELLY. TO THE NIECES AND NEPHEWS, AUNTS, UNCLES AND COUSINS. A SPECIAL HEARTFELT LOVE TO THE "OUTLAWS" (THE IN-LAWS!). TO OUR GRANDMA & FOR THE DAYS OF OUR LIVES.

I WONDER IF JULIA CHILD CAN HEAR THE ECHOES OF THE LAUGHTER AT THE MILLIONS OF DINNER PARTIES & WINE TASTINGS THAT SHE INSPIRED? SHE TAUGHT ME & ALL MY FRIENDS HOW TO COOK WHICH GAVE US SO MUCH. SHE CHANGED THE WORLD & SHE IS LOVED.

SUSAN
BRANCH
P.O. BOX 1468
SAN LUIS OBISPO,
CA 93406

I'LL PUT YOU ON MY
NEWSLETTER MAILING LIST!

COME VISIT MY WEBSITE
WWW.SUSANBRANCH.COM

INDEX

A
Appetizers, . . . 26-40
Avocado & Grape-
  fruit Spears, . . 36
BLT's, Baby, . . . 28
Chicken, Crunchy, . 30
Clams, Steamers, . 35
Cocktails, ... 114
Croutons, Butter-Bit, 34
Figs & Goat Cheese, 28
Fruit & Cheese w/
  Orange Dip, . . 36
Garlic Tomato Bread, 34
Gorgonzola Cream, 28
Halloween ideas, 119
Ideas, ... 26
Indian Shuck
  Bread, . . . 37
Mushrooms, Stuffed, 36
Mushrooms, Wild,
  on Toast, . . 28
Onion Rings, Red
  Chili, ... 29
Pears, Prosciutto, 28
Pecans, Spiced, . 27
Potato Bar, . . 29
Potatoes, Stuffed
  New, ... 32
Shrimp, Garlic, . 27
Shrimp, Sticky, . 31

Soup, Butternut
  Shotglass, . . . 33
Steamers, . . . 35
Apple(s)
  in Crisp, ... 95
  in Curried Squash, 51
  w/ Pork Chops, . 75
Asian
  Dipping Sauce, . . 31
  Sesame Ginger
    Shrimp, ... 81
  Sticky Shrimp, . 31
Avocado & Grape-
  fruit Spears, . 36

B
Balsamic Syrup, . 50
Banana(s)
  in French Eclair, 100
  & Gipsy Cream, 104
Bean(s)
  White, Salad, . . 48
  in Chili, ... 78
Beef
  in Chili, ... 78
  in Stew, . . . 77
  Tenderloin of, . 84
Beet Salad, Roasted, 45
Beverages
Cold
  Arnold Palmers, 85
  Halloween Punch, 118
  Harvest Moon, . . 114
  Vampire's Kiss, . 114
Hot
  Chocolate, . . . 111
  Cider, Spiced, . . 112
  Coffee, ... 113
  Eggnog Cappuccino, 113
  for Cold & Flu, . 112
  Kiss-in-the-Dark, 113
  Pumpkin Latte, . 113
Biscuits, Farmhouse, 60
Bourbon
  Ice Cream . . . 104

Mashed Sweet
  Potatoes, . . . 49
  Praline, . . . 104
Bread
  Biscuits, Farmhouse, . 60
  Corn Bread, Iowa, . 61
  Croutons, Butter-Bit, 34
  Garlic Tomato, . . 34
  Indian Shuck, . . 37
  Stuffing(s)
    for Pork Chops, . 75
    My Grandma's, . 64
Broccoli Slaw
    w/ Turkey, . . . 79
  Brownies, . . . 107
  Brussels Sprouts, . 50
Butter
  Bee (honey), . . 61
  Maple, ... 37
  Orange, . . . 109

C
Cake
  Cheese, Pumpkin, . 97
  Birthday
    (chocolate), . . 98
  Fortune, . . . 99
  Gingerbread, . . 93
Casserole(s)
  Corn Pudding, . . 54
  Macaroni & Cheese, 76
  Stuffed Pork Chops
    w/ Sweet Potatoes
    & Apples, . . 75
  Sweet Potato, . . 65
Chantilly (Whipped)
  Cream, ... 93
Cheese
  Blue, Dressing, . 45
  Fruit and, . . 36
  Figs & Goat, . . 28

Cheese (con't)
  Gorgonzola Cream, . .28
  Macaroni &,   76
Cheesecake, Pumpkin, 97
Chicken
  Crunchy, ... 30
  in Cream Sauce, . . 74
  Soup, French, . . 57
  Stock; ideas for
    use, . . . 56
Chili, Touchdown, .78
Chocolate
  Brownies, . . . 107
  Cake, . . .98
  Cocoa Mix, . . .111
  Eclair Wreath, . .100
  Glaze, . . . 101
  Hot, ... 111
  Sauce, ...103
Cider, Autumn Spiced,112
Cinnamon
  Ice Cream, . . .94
  Sugar, . . . 109
Clams, Steamers, . 35
Cocktails, ...114
Cocoa Mix, . . .111
Coffee. See
  Beverages, Hot
Cookies
  Cookie Cutter
    Ginger Crisps, .106
  in Ice Cream
    Sandwich, . 104
  Molasses, . . 105
Corn
  Bread, Iowa, . 61
  Chowder, . . 72
  Pudding, . 54
Crafts, . . . 18-19
  Cookie Man, . 21
  Embroidery, . .19
  Harvest Crown, 17
  Pin Cushion, . 19
  Placecards, 15
  Sachet, . 19
  Thanksgiving
    Centerpiece, . 69

Cranberry
  Apple Crisp, . . 95
  Sauce, ...69
Croutons
  Butter-Bit, . . 34
  w/ Tenderloin, . . 84

Decorating, ...10
  The Autumn Table, .14
  The Guest Room, . . 16
Desserts, . . 92-107
Dipping Sauce,
  Asian, . . . 31
  See also Sauce
Dressing. See Salad
  Dressing;
  See Stuffing
Drinks.
  See Beverages;
  See Cocktails

Eclair, French
  Wreath, ...100
Entertaining, . .12-13
  Eat, Drink &
    Be Scary, . . .119
  Napkin Folding, . 14
  Placecards, . 15
  The Autumn Table, .14
  The Guest Room, . 16
  'Tis the Season, . 118
  See also Menus

Figs & Goat Cheese, . . 28
Fish & Shellfish
  Clams, Steamers, . 35
  Salmon, Lime, . 80
  Scallops, Mashed
    Potatoes & Corn
    Chowder, . . 72
  Shrimp, Garlic, . 27
  Shrimp, in Potato
    Bugs, . . 82
  Shrimp, Sesame
    Ginger, . . 81
  Shrimp, Sticky, . 31

Fruit & Cheese, . 36
  See also Name of Fruit
Gardening
  Harvest, . . 38-39
  Mari-Gold-Dust, . 54
Garnishes, . . 42
  Balsamic Syrup, . 50
  Cookie Cutter Cutouts, 42-106
  Croutons, Butter-Bit, 34
  Garlic Tomato Bread, . 34
  Ginger Crisp Leaves, . 106
  Leek Frisée, . .80
  Mushroom, Wild
    Ragout, . . .53
  Onion Rings, Red
    Chili, . . .29
  Pecans, Spiced, . .27
  Potato Leaves, . .44
Gift Ideas
  Bourbon Praline, . 104
  Butter-Bit Croutons,34
  Chocolate Sauce, . 103
  Cranberry Sauce, . 69
  Cocoa Mix, . . .111
  Gift Baskets, . 20-21
  Halloween movies, . 119
  Mari-Gold-Dust, . 54
  Marshmallows,
    Homemade, . .110
  Pecans, Spiced, . 27
  Gingerbread Cake, . 93
  Ginger Crisps, . .106
  Goat Cheese, & Figs, 28
  Gravy, ...68

Ham, Indiana, &
  Sweet Potato Soup, .55
Halloween, . . . 115-119

Ice Cream
  Bourbon (Tipsy Cream),104
  Cinnamon, ...94
  Lemon Thyme, . . 38
  Sandwiches, Ginger
    Crisp, . . . 104
  Toasted Snowballs, 102

Icing, Royal, . . . 103

J
Jell-O, Rainbow, . . 67

L
Lamb
  Leg of, Crusted, . . 83
  Shanks, Braised, . 76
Leek Frisée, . . . 80
Lime Salmon, . . . 80

M
Macaroni &
  Cheese, . . . 76
Main Dishes, . . 72-84
Maple Butter, . . 37
Marshmallows,
  Homemade, . . . 110
Menus
  Autumn Picnic, . 85
  Elegant Dinner, . 84
  Halloween Dinner, 119
  Rainy Saturday
    Lunch, . . . 58
  Trick or Treat
    Dinner (children's), 118
Molasses Cookies, . 105
Mushroom(s)
  Stuffed, as
    Appetizer, . . 36
  Stuffed, as Side
    Dish, . . . 52
  Wild, Ragout, . 53
  Wild, on Toast, . 28

O
Onion
  Leek Frisée, . . 80
  Rings, Red Chili, 29
  Sauce, Caramelized, 43
Orange
  Butter, . . . 109
  Dip, . . . 36

P
Parties.
  See Entertaining;
  Menus
Pasta
  Macaroni & Cheese, 76

Pear(s)
  w/ Orange Dip, . 36
  w/ Prosciutto, . 28
  Red, in Salad, . . 47
  Salsa, . . . 50
  Tatin, . . . 92
Pecans
  in Salad, . . 47
  Spiced, . . 27
  Spinach Toss, . 46
Pork
  Chops, Stuffed, . 75
  Riblets, . . 32
Potato (es)
  Anna, . . . 44
  Baked, . . . 42
  Bar (Skins), . . 29
  Bugs, . . . 82
  Buttermilk, Mashed, 49
  Leaves, . . 44
  Stuffed, New, . 32
  See also Sweet Potato
Prosciutto Pears, . 28
Pudding
  Corn, . . . 54
  Indian, . . 96
Pumpkin
  as containers, 51, 77, 119
  Cheesecake, . . 97
  Curried, Pots (Jack-
    Be-Little), . 51
  Latte, . . . 113
Punch, Halloween, . 118

R
Radicchio, Roasted
  w/ Turkey Bacon, 50
Ribs. See Pork
Rice, Happy, . . 74
Royal Icing, . . 103

S
Salad
  Beet, Roasted, . 45
  Pear, Grape &
    Pecan, . . 47
  Spinach, Pecan
    Toss, . . . 46

  White Bean, Warm,
    w/ Sage & Garlic, 48
Salad Dressing
  Blue Cheese, . . 45
Salmon, Lime, . . 80
Salsa, Pear, . . 50
Sandwich
  BLT's, Baby, . . 28
Sauce
  Balsamic Syrup
    (Reduction), . . 50
  Bourbon Praline, . 104
  Chocolate, . . 103
  Cranberry, . . 69
  Hollandaise, . . 42
  Lemon, . . . 93
  Onion, Caramelized, 43
  Orange, for Fruit, 36
Scallops, Mashed Potatoes
  & Corn Chowder, . 72
Scones, Cream, . . 109
Seafood. See Fish; also
  name of Fish or
  Shellfish
Shrimp
  in Potato Bugs, . 82
  Garlic, . . . 27
  Sesame Ginger, . 81
  Sticky, . . 31
Side Dishes, . . 42-61
  for Thanksgiving, 64-69
Soup
  Butternut, . . 33
  Chicken, French, . 57
  Chicken Stock, . 56
  Corn Chowder, . 72
  Ham & Sweet
    Potato, . . 55
  Tomato, . . 58
Squash
  Acorn, . . . 42
  Butternut Soup, . 33
  Curried Pumpkin
    Pots, . . 51
Spaghetti, Parmesan, 52
Spaghetti, w/ Shrimp, 81

Stew, Harvest, ... 77
Stock, Chicken, . . . 56
Stuffing
  for Pork Chops, . . . 75
  My Grandma's, . 64
Sweets. See Desserts
Sweet Potato (es)
  Bourbon Mashed, 49
  Casserole, . . 65
  Ham &, Soup, . 55

Tatin, Pear, ... 92
Tea, Afternoon, . . 108
  Scones, . . . 109
Thanksgiving, . . 62
  Recipes for, . 64–69
Turkey
  about, ... 68
  in the Straw, . 79
  Hot, Sandwich, 60

Vegetables
  Roasted, Fall . . 43
  w/ Hollandaise, . 42
See also name of Vegetable

WISHES

MAY GOD IN HIS WISDOM
AND INFINITE LOVE,
LOOK DOWN ON YOU ALWAYS
FROM HEAVEN ABOVE.
MAY HE SEND YOU GOOD FORTUNE,
CONTENTMENT & PEACE,
AND MAY ALL YOUR BLESSINGS
FOREVER INCREASE.

When does writing have an end? What is the
warning sign? A trembling of the
hand? Colette

In Love with Nature